Detroit Monographs in Musicology/Studies in Music, No. 27

Editor
J. Bunker Clark
University of Kansas

Arndt Mehring

Friedrich Kuhlau in the Mirror of His Flute Works

Edited by
Jane Rausch

Translated from the German by
Laszlo and Doris Tikos

HARMONIE PARK PRESS
Warren, Michigan ◆ 2000

This book was originally published in 1992 by
Zimmermann-Frankfurt under the title
Friedrich Kuhlau im Speigel seiner Flötenwerke

Printed and bound in the United States of America
Published by
Harmonie Park Press
23630 Pinewood
Warren, Michigan 48091

Production Manager, Elaine J. Gorzelski
Editor and Index, J. Bunker Clark
Book design, Colleen McRorie
Cover design, Mitchell Groters

Library of Congress Cataloging-in-Publication Data

Mehring, Arndt, 1963-
[Friedrich Kuhlau im Spiegel seinter Flötenwerke. English]
Friedrich Kuhlau in the mirror of his flute works / Arndt Mehring ; edited by Jane Rausch ; translated from the German by Laszlo and Doris Tikos.
p. cm. -- (Detroit monographs in musicology/Studies in music / no. 27)
"Flute compositions by Friedrich Kuhlau": p.
Includes bibliographical references (p.) and index.
ISBN 0-89990-091-7
1. Kuhlau, Friedrich, 1786-1832. Instrumental music. I. Rausch, Jane M. II. title. III. Series.

ML410.K96 M4413 2000
788.3'2'092--dc21

"I promise to change hate to love
through the sweet song of my flute."

— from Friedrich Kuhlau's
Magic Flute opera *Lulu*

Contents

Illustrations

Music Examples

Examples

Examples

Editor's Preface

For many years musicologists asserted that because of lack of interest by the so-called major composers of the early nineteenth century—Mozart, Weber, Schubert, and Beethoven—"early 19th century flute music consisted of salon pieces and variations of no great musical interest or else chamber music by a relatively few composers of second rank."[1] During the past twenty years, however, this mistaken notion has been thoroughly refuted by the rediscovery and publication of many excellent sonatas, concertos and fantasias by François Devienne, Theodore Boehm, Jules Demerssemann, Anton Reicha, Anton Bernhard Fürstenau, and especially by those of Daniel Friedrich Kuhlau (1786-1832), a native-born German who spent most of his life in Denmark and who wrote more than thirty opus numbers in which he provided parts for at least one flute.

Regrettably, the growing accessibility of music scores written by these "second tier" composers has not been accompanied by serious academic studies of their lives and careers. Biographies of Mozart, Donizetti, and Beethoven fill the library shelves, but for information regarding lesser composers, the English reader is limited to consulting the accurate but compressed entries in *New Grove*. Given this situation, an English translation of Arndt Mehring's *Kuhlau im Spiegel seiner Flötenwerke*, based upon a wide variety of German and Danish sources, promises to be a great boon to flutists interested in early Romantic music, for in addition to providing a biography of this extraordinary musician, Mehring offers an expert's analysis of all of his flute pieces as well as advice as to how best to play them in the manner envisioned by the composer. When coupled with an awareness of Kuhlau's ability to overcome adversity in life and of his tragic death at the age of 46, Mehring's valuable commentary

[1] Howard Mayer Brown, "Flute, §5: Repertory and its history," *The New Grove Dictionary of Music and Musicians* (Cambridge: Macmillan, 1982), 6:680.

cannot help but deepen the flutist's ability to perform his engaging works. As one explores Kuhlau's sonatas, duets, trios, and quartets, one soon realizes the truth of Leonardo De Lorenzo's assertion, originally written in 1951:

> There is one supreme virtue in the music of Kuhlau, it never palls; on the contrary, one may play it every day, year after year, without its losing its freshness, and the more intimately one becomes acquainted with it, the more strongly one becomes impressed with the genius of its illustrious composer. . . .[2]

For this English edition, I have updated the catalog of Kuhlau's flute works, originally compiled by Mehring in 1992. For example, the current list now indicates that op. 94, "Variations on a Theme from Onslow's *Le Colporteur*," and op. 99, "Introduction and Variations on 'Toujours de mon juene âge' from *Le Colporteur*," both for flute and piano, out of print since 1828, have been reissued by Zimmermann in new editions in 1995—thanks to the efforts of Mehring. It also includes some suspect editions such as op. 13b, Three Concert Duos, arranged (with piano) by Moyse, and op. 57b, Three Duos, for two flutes, published by Billaudot, which Mehring believes are not original.

I would like to thank my colleagues at the University of Massachusetts: Pamela Juengling, Albert Huetteman, and Frank Hugus for their help in clarifying some obscure details in the German and Danish texts, and also Peggy McKinnon for her expert assistance in preparing the manuscript. Finally, I am grateful to Harmonie Park Press for accepting this project, and especially to J. Bunker Clark for his superb editing skills which transformed what had been a labor of love by amateur devotees into a solid piece of music history.

Jane M. Rausch

University of Massachusetts, Amherst
December 1999

---

[2] De Lorenzo, *My Complete Story of the Flute: The Instrument, the Performer, the Music*, rev. and expanded ed. (Lubbock: Texas Tech University Press, 1992), 109.

Translators' Note

The translators have made no attempt to reproduce the style of Kuhlau's letters or that of other contemporary documents written in early nineteenth-century German or Danish, but instead have used contemporary, standard English.

Introduction

Friedrich Kuhlau's life (1786-1832) encompasses almost exactly the time period known today as the era of German Romanticism. Politically delineated by the two French Revolutions, the era is divided into two epochs by the Congress of Vienna of 1815: the first being the Napoleonic Empire, and the second, the Restoration and the social predominance of Vienna. These political and social events had decisive influence upon Kuhlau's life and work. Because of Napoleon's struggle for power, Kuhlau became a political refugee in 1810, and his two visits to the cultural center of Vienna in 1821 and 1825 provided him with important inspiration for his work.

Among Kuhlau's 127 opuses, the dramatic compositions were considered the most important during his lifetime, while most of the commissioned chamber music pieces, written for the "more advanced friends of music,"[1] were dismissed as second class "salon pieces." Even in 1886, Carl Thrane, his first biographer, wrote: "Had Kuhlau enjoyed a regular yearly income, which would have provided him with a decent living, a considerable portion of his compositions would not have come into existence."[2] While it is correct to say that Kuhlau wrote some of his works to alleviate his eternal financial problems, it would be wrong to assume that many of these compositions, especially those for the flute, were second-rate, as Karl Graupner stated in his dissertation written in 1930: "This is why you find so many insignificant pieces among his flute compositions."[3] The fact is that Kuhlau made more money with the thirty opus numbers in which he provided parts for a least one flute than with all of his other compositions.

---

[1] *Die Musik in Geschichte und Gegenwart* (hereafter cited as MGG), 7 (1989): 1878.

[2] Carl Thrane, *Friedrich Kuhlau*, German translation of *Danske Komponister* (Leipzig: Breitkopf & Härtel, 1886), 50.

[3] Karl Graupner, "Friedrich Kuhlau" (Ph.D. diss., University of Munich, 1930), 53.

The fact that during the first half of the nineteenth century music publishers paid so generously for chamber music compositions for the flute can be explained by the large number of amateur flutists, who guaranteed the sale of suitable compositions. It was especially men who bragged that they could play the "magic baton" "to transport their own emotions into the wind of a melodious journey" as it is described so beautifully by Jean Paul (1763-1825) in his biography *Flegeljahre* (Adolescence): "I so like the . . . flute, the magic baton, which changes one's internal world, when it is touched by it; it is a divining rod plumbing the depths of the soul."[4]

Among the amateur flutists of this period were such people as Friedrich Hölderlin (1770-1834), who under the tutelage of the blind flutist Friedrich Ludwig Dulon "mastered the flute very skillfully,"[5] as well as Arthur Schopenhauer (1788-1860), who "found relaxation in his daily flute practice."[6] Among composers we find Hector Berlioz (1803-69), who for a while received lessons daily for two hours "in voice and flute,"[7] as well as Peter Ilich Tchaikovsky (1840-93), who confessed "I myself play the flute a little"[8]—but who actually played it so well that he himself took one part in Kuhlau's Flute Quartet, op. 103, in a concert in St. Petersburg in honor of Clara Schumann.[9] Johannes Brahms (1833-97), who owned a copy of the piano score of Kuhlau's *Lulu*, would have liked to learn the flute in order to be able to play Kuhlau's flute sonatas.[10]

The rapid dissemination of Kuhlau's flute music can be attributed on the one hand to the fact that, it was published during his lifetime, and on the other hand to the fact that in addition to its compositional value, it demonstrates a precise knowledge of the flute as an instrument. A comparison with the flute pieces of some of his contemporaries reveals that they do not have the same qualities. Despite the charm of the flute music written by Jean Louis Tulou (1786-1865), which lacks a certain quality of composition, and the sonatas of Friedrich Schneider (1786-1853), notwithstanding the technical excellence of individual movements, only Kuhlau possessed the precise knowledge necessary to be a first-class composer for flute. From Carl Maria von Weber (1786-1826), the most important composer of the period, unfortunately there is only one significant piece for flute extant, the Trio in G minor, op. 63. Weber, like many other romantic composers, was more interested in composing

---

[4] Jean Paul, *Flegeljahre: Eine Biographie* (Frankfurt a. M.: Insel, 1986), vol. 1, no. 13, 89.

[5] Ulrich Hässermann, *Friedrich Hölderlin in Selbzeugnissen und Bilddokumenten* (Reinbek bei Hamburg: Rowohit, 1961), 50.

[6] Walter Abendroth, *Schopenhauer* (Reinbeck bei Hamburg: Rowohit, 1988), 120.

[7] Wolfgang Dömling, *Hector Berlioz in Selbstzeugnissen und Bilddokumenten* (Reinbeck bie Hamburg: Rowohlt, 1977), p. 12.

[8] Tchaikovsky letter, 4 January 1880.

[9] Alja Rachmanowa (pseud. for Galina von Hoyer), *Tschaikowskij: Schicksal und Schaffen* (Vienna: Neff, 1972), 70.

[10] Ulrike von Hase-Schmundt, Notes to *Ausgewählte Flötenwerke* (Claves 50-8705).

music for the clarinet, because the possibilities of modulation in sound color of this woodwind instrument corresponded more readily to the romantic *zeitgeist.*

The extraordinary ability of Kuhlau to write music for the flute goes back to his early childhood experiences with this instrument. He listened to his father giving flute lessons at home, and he himself took up the flute as a child. Also, throughout his entire life he was in close contact with many flutists of his time. The numerous compositions by Kuhlau, written as if "tailor-made" for the flute, even resulted in his being incorrectly identified in contemporary descriptions, as the solo flutist of the Royal Orchestra in Copenhagen.[11] In 1829, at the time when he had already given up playing the flute to concentrate on composition, Kuhlau himself rejected this claim, with the following ominous sentence: ". . . and I can't play even the simplest position on the flute. . . ."[12] After his death this particular statement has been used to disprove his special relationship towards the flute, and thus to argue that his numerous works for this instrument were salon pieces of inferior quality.

Kuhlau's first biographer, Carl Thrane, followed this line of argument in 1886, when he described the flute as an instrument "which, by its very nature, must be considered to play a subordinate role."[13] But the reason he took this position was to rid Kuhlau of the nickname "the Beethoven of the Flute,"[14] and to present him rather as an important composer of substantial operas. His attempt failed, however, because Kuhlau's larger works could not compete with the compositions of his contemporaries. The resulting negative outcome was that some of Kuhlau's flute pieces were allowed to go out of print at that time. Nonetheless, almost all of his works are available today in new editions.

The author of this book considers himself very fortunate in having discovered original first editions of the last two flute pieces composed by Kuhlau, which had been missing from modern editions. As a result, for the first time in history, we possess all of Kuhlau's surviving flute pieces. This book is about the complete collection of his flute music, and analyzes the special features of these works. Included are numerous variation cycles, with the original themes, that are part of Kuhlau's flute music in order to provide important help in the interpretation of these compositions. Nordic folk songs, as well as orchestra and piano scores of long-forgotten operas, have been rediscovered for the purposes of this book.

In addition to the detailed discussions of individual works, Kuhlau's biography is presented as faithfully as possible, and always in connection with his flute compositions. For biographical data three sources are used: the biography Carl Thrane

---

[11] Adolph Goldberg, *Porträts und Biographien hervorrangender Flöten-Virtuosen, -Dilettanten und -Komponisten* (Berlin, 1906; reprint, Celle: Moeck, 1987).

[12] Letter to W. C. Müller, 1 December 1829, in Gorn Busk, *Kuhlau Breve view alle folgenden Kuhlaubriefe* (Copenhagen: Engstrøm & Sødring, 1990) (hereafter cited as Busk), 146-47.

[13] Thrane, 48.

[14] *MGG*, 7:1878.

wrote in 1886, which is based mostly on anecdotes and conjectures; the dissertation written by Karl Graupner in 1930, which is more scholarly than Thrane's work but still in many places falls back upon Thrane's unsupported information; and the excellent dissertation by Gorm Busk, written in Danish in 1986, which examines the individual periods of Kuhlau's life very accurately. All of these biographies share one common feature: they emphasize Kuhlau's life from the point of view of his operas and pay little attention to his flute compositions (Thrane and Graupner not at all, while Busk deals with them only marginally).

This book focuses on the neglected areas. I have tried to present the genesis and effectiveness of Kuhlau's flute compositions, which, in my opinion, are the basis for the significance and lasting renown of this musician.

Arndt Mehring

Mönchengladbach, Germany
1992

Friedrich Kuhlau in the Mirror of His Flute Works

FRIEDRICH KUHLAU

Lithograph by Emil Baerentzen

Courtesy Konigliche Bibliothek Kopenhagen
(Wintherthur: Amadeus Verlag, 1981)

1

Uelzen, Lüneburg, Altona, Braunschweig, 1786-1802: The First Flute Compositions

Friedrich Daniel Rudolf Kuhlau was born on 11 September 1786 in Uelzen, a small provincial town situated between Hannover and Hamburg. The idyllic town in the Lüneburger Heide (moorland) belonged at that time to the electorate of Hannover, which had been in a personal union with England from 1714, and since 1760 had been ruled by the British King George III. At that time the military regiments stationed in the Hannover electorate had been reinforced because the British were expecting further attacks from their archenemy France, which had occupied a large part of the territory in 1757 including Uelzen.[1] The Twelfth Regiment of the "Von Linsing" Infantry was stationed there in 1786, and Kuhlau's father, Johann Karl Kuhlau (1747-1830), was employed in it as a military musician. According to the scant information we have of him, he was simple and not very well-educated, but he was a devoted family man, who tried to improve his rather meager military pay by giving music lessons so that he could provide for his wife and children.[2] In 1770 he married Dorothea Charlotte Seegers (1752-1830) of Hannover, and they had eleven children, of whom only five survived—three sons and two daughters. Friedrich, baptized in Uelzen's St. Mary's Church on 13 September 1786 two days after his birth, was the youngest of the boys. From the very beginning of his life he was accustomed to hearing the sounds of the flute during the music lessons conducted by his father.

Kuhlau's father was a "Hoboist" or "Hautboist" (as all military musicians in Germany were called up until 1918, with the exception of trumpet players and drummers who received higher pay and were held in greater esteem because they

---

[1] Hans E. Seidat, ed., *Der Landkreis Uelzen* (Uelzen, 1981), 44.

[2] Karl Graupner, "Friedrich Kuhlau," 16.

formed part of the Communication and Signal units), and he played flute as well as the oboe.[3] When his regiment was relocated in 1793, the family moved to Lüneburg, where three years later Friedrich suffered an accident with grave consequences. As biographer Carl Thrane writes:

> He was about nine and a half years old and living with his parents in Lüneburg, when one evening he was sent out in the dark with a bottle to fetch something. He stopped in front of the window of a shoemaker, where an especially pretty lamp had drawn his attention. He went up a few steps to take a closer look at the lamp, when he heard someone calling his name. As he hurried down the stairs, he stumbled and hit his head against the bottle, which shattered into splinters of glass that penetrated his right eye.[4]

Dr. Meidel, who was called, could not save the eye, and the injuries were so severe that young Friedrich had to stay in bed for a long time. In May 1796, about four months after the accident, his concerned father wrote in a letter to Amalie Kuhlau (1774-1851), Friedrich's oldest sister:

> Fritz is still the same as you saw him the last time, and Dr. Meidel says that everything must take its due course; otherwise he will not improve. He might even get a high temperature, and only after that will things be all right. But it is a bad situation. Yesterday my friends and I, who were here on furlough, received orders to report to the regiment immediately. . . . Dr. Meidel has just arrived to change Fritz's bandages. We saw with the greatest anguish that Fritz's eye was protruding out of his head. Dr. Meidel says that this is the best that can be done, and that Fritz will not look so dreadful once the wounds heal. . . .[5]

Just how "dreadful" Fritz looked after his long recuperation is difficult to say nowadays. The existing pictures and drawings that we have of him either show only the left side of his profile, or idealize his appearance according to the fashion of the times. However, his appearance and his remarkable height later had an extraordinary effect upon his contemporaries. One of them, Moritz Adolph Schlesinger, wrote to Beethoven: "He is a Cyclops. His one eye is close to his nose."[6] His extraordinary

---

[3] MGG, 9:315.

[4] Thrane, 2 ff.

[5] Letter from J. C. Kuhlau to Amalie Kuhlau, 7 May 1796, in Gorm Busk, *Friedrich Kuhlau: En biografi og en kritisk analyse af hans musikdramatiske production* (Ph.D. diss., Kobenhavns Universitet; Aarhus: Publimus, Engstrom & Sodring, 1986).

[6] Letter from Schlesinger to Beethoven in Alexander Wheelock Thayer, *Ludwig van Beethovens Leben*, 2nd ed., 5 vols. (1872-79; reprint, Hildesheim: Olms, 1970-72), 5:234ff.

appearance and that he cared for his parents for a long period of time may be responsible for many of his characteristics. A shy and solitary person, he was a bachelor his entire life, who later selflessly took care of his parents for sixteen years. He himself called the accident "at anytime an extraordinary stroke of luck" that had a decisive influence upon his fate. "He used to assure us that he could read the notes as well with one eye, as others do with two."[7] He used to say that because of this extraordinary luck his parents placed a piano over his bed as a diversion, and he found for the first time in his life enjoyment in music, and that his parents recognized his musical talent. The close connection between the consequences of the accident and his becoming a musician is indicated in a letter he wrote to his sister when he was almost ten years old:

> Nothing is really the matter with me except that my head is bashed in and the hole in my cheek has been filled. I have already used up twelve stone jars of *Latwerge* but now no more. Soon I should received some new beautiful arias, and as soon as I have them, I will copy them and send them to you. . . .[8]

His parents recognized his musical talent from his improvised piano music, and they tried to support him in developing it as much as they could within their limited financial means. His first piano teacher was Hartwig Ahrenbostel, the organist of the Holy Ghost Church (Heiligen-Geist-Kirche) in Lüneburg, and his father himself gave him lessons on the flute. Friedrich was thus ten years old when he learned to play the flute—a fact his biographers mention, but try to discount by making references to two quotations from his letters. The first of them was written seventeen years later in 1813: ". . . I play this instrument only a little but I know it very well. . . ."[9] The other letter was written another sixteen years later in 1829: ". . . and I can't play even the simplest position on the flute. . . ."[10]

Considering the large lapse of time between these two statements, we can assume that Kuhlau seem to have gradually given up playing the flute so that he could devote himself completely to his compositions. This conclusion is supported by the fact that in later years he also gave up public piano performances in favor of his creative work: ". . . since I'm not a concert musician any more. . . ."[11] What is important though, is to remember that Kuhlau's ability to compose splendidly for the flute was based above all on his past experiences as a flute player. The fact

---

[7] Ibid.

[8] Letter to Amalie Kuhlau, 7 May 1796, in Busk, 25. *Latwerge* was a medicinal preparation made with sugar and syrup or honey. —Ed.

[9] Letter to G. C. Härtel, 4 March 1813, in Busk, 49-50.

[10] Letter to M. C. Müller, December 1829, in Busk, 46-47.

[11] Letter to J. M. Witkowsky, 5 May 1829, in Busk, 132-33.

that his flute music is far above the contemporary compositions of flute virtuosi derives from his training as a piano player and composer.

His first flute compositions—which are not extant any more—were dances and smaller pieces written while he was still in Lüneburg. Thrane explains:

> It happened that one day he visited this green grocer who himself was a passionate flutist. The merchant used this opportunity to ask the boy if he could get some sheet music from his father who besides the violin (!) was also a flute player. Whether the young Fritz did not find the sheet music, or he found it to be more interesting to write them himself, we do not know, but he composed some dances, and some smaller pieces for the flute which he passed on to the merchant.[12]

For payment he supposedly received a "huge bag of raisins and almonds," which taught him that one could make money by composing flute music.[13] Of course, young Friedrich could not foresee yet that his flute compositions would bring him more money than all his other works put together, including his operas.

Since his father's military unit was stationed at different places after 1796, first in Northeim, then in Osterode, and then in Göttingen, and since the family could not constantly change its domicile, Kuhlau was sent to different boarding schools to finish his education, which he had started together with his brother Andreas (1782-1858) in Lüneburg. On 28 June 1800 he matriculated at the Christeaneum,[14] a Latin boarding school in Altona, where he participated in the musical programs of the school.

On 2 April 1802 he was registered as a First Form pupil in the Katherineum, a high school in Braunschweig, where, according to the curriculum, he received a well-rounded education which included Latin, German, mathematics, geometry, trigonometry, science, religion, and ethics.[15] He earned his tuition and his living as a *Kurrendeschüler*[16] by singing in the church choir. It was also his duty to go from house to house to collect the voluntary payments, which at that time constituted the teachers' salaries. Additionally, he gave music lessons to two of the minister's sons.

In Braunschweig Kuhlau became acquainted with the opera, which was under French direction and had on the playbill, among other works, operas by Mozart, Gluck, Cherubini, and Boieldieu. It is not inconceivable that Kuhlau participated in these productions, either in the extra choir provided by his school's pupils or possibly as a flutist in the orchestra. It was here that Kuhlau made the acquaintance of Louis Spohr (1784-1859), who was two years his junior, and played the violin. The friendship

---

[12] Thrane, 5.

[13] Ibid.

[14] Busk, 22.

[15] Graupner, 16.

[16] A *Kurrendeschüler* was a poor boy who sang on the street for bread. —Trans.

Johann Karl Kuhlau
(oboist)
b. 5 June 1747 in Leipzig
d. 21 January 1830 in Lyngbye

Charlotte Dorothea Kuhlau b. Seergern
(*1752)
d. 13 November 1830 in Lyngbye

Johann Caspar Friedrich b. 23 July 1772 in Stade	Sophie Clara Amalie b. 23 August 1774 in Stade d. 8 February 1851 in Leipzig	Anna Sophia Catharina b. 2 October 1770 in Stade	David Gottfried Martin (musician in Calcutta) b. 2 May 1780 in Stade, d.?	Johann Andreas Christian (salesman) b. 25 September 1782 in Stade d. 22 September 1858 in Leipzig	Hanna Margarethe Wilhelmine b. 13 March 1785 in Uelzen d. 11 July 1785 in Uelzen	Friedrich Daniel Rudolph (composer) b. 11 September 1786 in Uelzen d. 12 March 1832 in Copenhagen	Catharina Dorothea b. 25 June 1789 in Uelzen	Christina Louise Magdalene b. 20 January 1793 in Uelzen d. 24 January 1862 in Leipzig

KUHLAU'S PARENTS AND HIS SIBLINGS

of the two composers was emphasized later by Kuhlau when his dedicated his *Grande Sonate für Violine und Klavier*, op. 33, to Spohr. Kuhlau also met here the Bohemian composer Johann Ladislaus Dussek (1760-1812). Whether he took instrumental lessons in Braunschweig cannot be documented. Among the compositions he wrote here are several arias which he submitted for publication to the German music publisher Gottfried Christoph Härtel (1763-1827) with a letter explaining: "For a while now my friends have urged me to present some of my compositions for publication. But always I had to face the swords of the critics. But I'm not resisting my friends' request anymore, and therefore I beseech you to satisfy my most ardent desire to publish these arias."[17] Even though Härtel rejected his request at that time, between 1810 and 1822, he was to become Kuhlau's most important publisher.

Kuhlau stayed in Braunschweig no longer than a year and a half. From there he moved to Hamburg, probably at the beginning of 1803, where in the meantime his parents had also settled. His father had retired from the military and made a living as a music and instrumental teacher. In this northern German musical city Kuhlau set out to develop the most important impressions that he had received in Braunschweig, especially from the performances of Mozart's operas. It was here that his most fervent desire to became a composer, especially of dramatic works, came to fruition.

---

[17] Letter to Härtel, 12 January 1802, in Busk, 29.

2

HAMBURG, 1803-10: *VARIATIONS ET CAPRICES*, OP. 10 (BIS)

Hamburg must have appeared to Kuhlau very much the same as Charles Burney (1726-1814) experienced it during his musical journey in 1772:

> The streets are ill built, ill paved and narrow, but crowded with people who seem occupied with their own concerns; and there is an air of chearfulness [*sic*], industry, plenty, and liberty, seldom to be seen in other parts of Germany.[1]

Even though the town with its 13,000 inhabitants was a center for international business and banking, its musical life, once quite lively, was showing a decline in these years. As Burney remarked, "The town of Hamburg has been famous for its operas for a long time."[2] But the cultural life of the town had peaked, and Vienna had become the new center of European art. The time of Georg Philipp Telemann (1681-1767) and of his godson Carl Philipp Emanuel Bach (1714-88), who worked there as musical director from 1767 until his death and transformed Hamburg into a center of the so-called pre-Classic period, was irretrievably over. Even though Bach's successor Christian Friedrich Gottlieb Schwencke (1767-1822) was an excellent pianist and theoretician, he could not lead the town's musical life out of the petrified time of "sentimentality."

---

[1] Charles Burney, *Tagebuch einer musikalischen Reise durch Frankreich und Italien, durch Flandern, die Niederlande und am Rhein bis Wien, durch Böhmen, Sachsen, Brandenburg, Hamburg und Holland, 1770-1772*, ed. Eberhardt Klemm (Wilhelmshaven: Heinrichshofen, 1980), 438. Originally published in English as *The Present State of Music in France and Italy* (London, 1771) and *The Present State of Music in Germany, the Netherlands, and United Provinces* (London, 1773), and soon translated to German by Christophe Daniel Ebeling and Johann Joachim Christoph Bode.

[2] Ibid.

Schwencke was an accompanist for Bach, and a pupil of Johann Philipp Kirnberger (1721-83), who had studied mathematics and philosophy in Halle before he accepted the position of music director of Hamburg, succeeding Bach, on 1 October 1789. He was twenty-three years old, respected as a demanding teacher, and feared as a scathing critic. Kuhlau, who had a difficult time getting established in the former cultural center, tried first to make a living by giving piano lessons, since concert engagements in Hamburg were practically dependent on the benevolence of Schwencke. Concerning his situation as a performing artist Kuhlau wrote to his brother:

> When my only friend, Lichtenfeld[3] . . . and I think about our position as artists in Hamburg, it appear to be so pitiable . . . you can not even imagine it. We are disgusted with ourselves, that here in Hamburg . . . we will NEVER . . . NEVER . . . do anything important . . . and that I'll always remain—provided our situation doesn't change—a destitute piano teacher . . . and will never get any higher (as I would rather do!). . . . Thus, both of us have indigestion from this endlessly same repast, from this dear, blessed Hamburg, and unfortunately, we can easily foresee a total constipation of this short-live colon . . . well, both of us are ready to turn our backsides, or I should rather say, our backs on Hamburg, and see what the world looks like in some other places.[4]

Kuhlau and Lichtenfeld got as far as Bremen, where they gave a concert together. However, they spent all their honorarium there and therefore had to walk back to Hamburg.

The situation changed for the better when Kuhlau became a pupil of Schwencke. The famous music director's connections and the status of being one of his few pupils were decisive in order to receive concert engagements and to be published as a composer. Kuhlau, who came from the musically backward provinces, had great difficulty getting used to the tough demands of Schwencke during the first lessons. Every piece he presented to Schwencke was invariably judged as "utterly useless."[5] Schwencke's ire was further aroused when he caught Kuhlau red-handed as he was secretly touching a pipe that Schwencke considered "sacred." Kuhlau, who in the presence of women, had always been described as a quiet and timid person, had been dared to pick up the pipe by some teasing girls in Schwencke's house. Only after many lessons did Schwencke change his opinion. Once when Kuhlau submitted to him some manuscripts and was expecting the usual judgment "utterly useless," suddenly Schwencke said to him, "Herr Kuhlau, help yourself to a pipe!"[6] Kuhlau

---

[3] Lichtenfeld was a singer with the Hamburg Opera. —Ed.

[4] Letter to Andreas Kuhlau, 1803 (1802?), in Busk, 32-33.

[5] Thrane, 12.

[6] Ibid.

remembered this incident until the end of his life and often recounted it to his friends, but whether it was the true reason for his excessive fondness for pipe-smoking can not be established.

Concert announcements that are extant testify that between 1804 and 1810 Kuhlau gave regular performances in Hamburg as a pianist and composer. Two of these concerts which he presented along with flute virtuosi of the period can still be documented. On 15 March 1806, Kuhlau gave a concert together with Frederica Brincks,[7] and on 2 January 1808 he gave a recital with the flutist Cestenoble. In addition to a (now lost) symphony of Kuhlau, the program featured a *Varationen für das Fortepiano und die Flöte*, also not extant.

Entertainment Announcement
From 1 April 1805 to 31 March 1806

1. Vocal and Instrumental Concert by the Flute Virtuoso Dem. Búnck on 15 March 1806
4. Concert for the Fortepiano, composed and played by Herrn Kuhlau

Entertainment Announcement
From 1 April 1807 to 31 March 1808

At the Benefice-Vocal and Instrumental Concert
By Herrn Ritzenfeldt,
Played this Saturday the 2nd of January 1808

First part
1. Symphony by Kuhlau
5. Variations for the Pianoforte and the Flute, composed by Herrn Kuhlau
Executed by Herrn Kuhlau and Cestenoble

CONCERT ANNOUNCEMENTS, 1805 AND 1808, BY THE CITY OF HAMBURG

This was also the time when the first compositions of Kuhlau were published by several small music publishers. In June 1806 a certain Rudolphus in Altona and Hardieck in Hamburg announced the publication of *Rondo und Walzer für 2 Flöten*. However, this piece, as well as another early work, *Sonate für Klavier mit Flöte*, has disappeared.[8]

The first published and extant original works is *Variations et Solos pour le flute seule composés par F. Kuhlau*, op. 10. These twelve solo pieces enjoyed such a great popularity at the time that soon the Hamburg music publisher August Heinrich

---

[7] According to Busk, *Friedrich Kuhlau*, 26.

[8] Ibid., 27.

Cranz (1789-1870) brought out a new edition, announced in the *Allgemeine musikalische Zeitung* in June 1823 as "new editions of this composer's early music."[9] This edition utilized the engraving plate of the first edition, but with a new sequence of the pieces and a new title, *Variations et Caprices*, which served also as the basis for Peter Reidemeister's modern edition, which as yet has not been sufficiently appreciated. All twelve pieces have a performance time of not more than five minutes, and are—in terms of difficulty—much less demanding than Kuhlau's later flute music. For this reason, they are especially suitable as introductory studies to the work of this Romantic flute music. The range is *d´* to *g´´´*, the keys use up to three sharps and flats (both A major and C minor appear only once), and the incorporation of well-known arias and contemporary popular songs in seven of these pieces easily explain their popularity at the time. With the exception of the Duettino between Röschen and Felsenherz, "Nel cor più non mi sente" (All the joys escape me) from the second act of Giovanni Paisiello's (1740-1816) opera *La molinara* (The miller), used also by Theobald Boehm,[10] Johann Baptist Vanhal,[11] and Friedrich Silcher[12] as a theme for flute variations, the other melodies have by now been forgotten.

We were able to trace down the themes for no. 4 and no. 8. No. 4, "Es kann schon nicht alles so bleiben" (Things can not stay like that forever), is a melody by Friedrich Heinrich Himmel with a text by Auguste von Kotzubue:

Es kann ja nicht immer so bleiben	Things can not stay like that forever
Hier unter dem wechselndem Mond;	Here, under the changeable moon;
Es blueht eine Zeit und verwelket,	Everything that lives with us on earth
Was mit uns die Erde bewohnt.	Has its time of bloom and then will perish.[13]

No. 8, "Was ist der Mensch," is a guitar song by J. L. Evers written in 1795 with the following text:

Was ist der Mensch? Halb Tier, halb Engel	What then is man? Half beast, half angel
Klein, elend, duerftig—herrlich gross.	Small, needful, miserable, and wonderfully great
Was ist sein Schicksal? Tausent Mängel	What is his fate? Thousand needs
Und tausend Güter sind sein Los.	And thousand goods are his fate.[14]

---

[9] Peter Reidemeister, foreword to new edition of Kuhlau, *Variations et Caprices*, op. 10 (bis), (Winterthur: Amadeus, 1981).

[10] *Variationen für Flöte und Klavier*, op. 4.

[11] *Variationen für Flöte und Gitarre*, op. 42.

[12] *Variationen für Flöte und Klavier*.

[13] Reidemeister, ibid.

[14] Ibid.

During his Hamburg period Kuhlau composed, along with these twelve flute pieces, op. 10 (bis) (which should not be confused with *Duos concertantes* of the same opus number), several piano pieces, songs, and his major work, Piano Concerto in C major, op. 7. Kuhlau wrote this concerto under the influence of the Piano Concerto, op. 15, no. 1, in the same key, by Beethoven. He borrowed the contrast-rich orchestration between wind instruments, strings, and trumpets from the beginning of Beethoven's first movement, whose works he studied with his teacher, Schwencke, who had an especially appreciation for Beethoven. However, in public concerts in Hamburg, Beethoven's music was not frequently performed because he was considered to be too avant-garde (!). Works by Wolfgang Amadeus Mozart, Luigi Cherubini, and Joseph Haydn were preferred. Haydn's oratorio *Die Schöpfung* (The creation) had reached Hamburg by 1801.[15]

After 1810 Kuhlau's Piano Concerto, op. 7, could no longer be performed in Hamburg, because at the end of that year Kuhlau hastily fled the city for Copenhagen. What happened was exactly what Beethoven already in 1804 had been afraid of, when, after the crowning of Napoleon as emperor, he deleted the dedication "written for Bonaparte" from his *Eroica* Symphony. Napoleon's aggression and military policies turned nearly the entire middle of Europe into a French zone of occupation. Eventually it included north Germany, which was unwilling to recognize the so-called Decree of Mailand, a more stringent continental blockade against England, because it was afraid of an economic crisis caused by the interruption of trade in colonial products. The occupation of Hamburg by General Mortier led to massive unemployment and further stagnation of the city's cultural life. New soldiers, who at first were supposed to be volunteers, were recruited everywhere. In November 1810 the newspaper *Hamburgische Correspondent*, under the headline "Calling Up of Conscripts," summoned "all young men, born between 1785 and 1789 to enlist within four weeks."[16] A little later the *Hamburger Anzeiger* wrote "If you don't enlist, you will run the risk of losing everything you have, and you'll be ordered to the units with the earliest marching orders."[17]

Because of these threats, which had to be taken seriously, Kuhlau was afraid that—despite his impaired eyesight—he might also be drafted, perhaps as a military musician (flutist!). The nearest possible secure place was Denmark, which being an ally of France in the Coalition wars, had been attacked twice by the British who bombarded Copenhagen for three days in September 1807—and for this reason had been spared by France. Another incentive for Kuhlau to flee to Denmark was that King Friedrich VI, the reigning monarch since 1808, was considered to be a friend of the arts. Perhaps Kuhlau also had in mind his uncle Johann Daniel Kuhlau (1744-1810),

---

[15] MGG, 5:1400.

[16] *Hamburgischer Correspondent*, 17 and 28 November 1810.

[17] Thrane, 15.

who had emigrated to Aalborg in Denmark and enjoyed a regular income there as an organist. To earn a living in Denmark also became the greatest problem for Kuhlau, for, with the exception of some engagements, he never—for the rest of his life—left his adopted homeland.

3

Copenhagen, 1810-21: Duos, op. 10; Trios, op. 13

In December 1810 a certain German musician, calling himself "Kasper Meier," sought a safe haven in the old part of Copenhagen, which still lay in ruins after the British bombardment. Here in this city, which was one of the most important Scandinavian commercial ports, musical life in the eighteenth century had experienced a strong impetus that had reached a peak in 1748 when the Royal Theater was established. Three immigrant German musicians contributed to this development: Johann Ernst Hartmann (1726-93), who set to music two operettas by Johannes Ewald, *Balders Död* (1778) and *Fiskerne* (1780), and by so doing promoted popular interest in theater themes connected with the mythology of Nordic gods and spirits; Johann Abraham Peter Schulz (1747-1800), who as Capellmeister (director) had a decisive influence upon the Copenhagen orchestra; and Friedrich Ludwig Ämilius Kunzen (1761-1817), who as a composer elevated the quality of musical activities with his opera *Holger Danske* (1789), after Wieland's *Oberon*, and as Capellmeister by his frequent presentations of numerous Mozart operas, including *Così fan tutte* and *Don Giovanni*.

These musical activities in Copenhagen were supported by Denmark's king, Friedrich VI (1768-1839), who succeeded to the throne in 1808 after the death of his deranged father, Christian VII. Under his enlightened reign Danish literature flourished anew. Jens Immanuel Beggesen (1764-1826) and Johan Ludvig Heiberg (1791-1860) should be mentioned in this connection—both were engaged in a literary controversy with Adam Gottlob Oehlenschläger (1779-1850), the most important representative of Danish romanticism, who was of German origin. All three of them later wrote librettos for Kuhlau's compositions.

Around 1810 "Kasper Meier" came to live in a small room in the attic of the house where Oehlenschläger lived;[1] and only after several weeks' stay in Copenhagen

[1] Thrane, 15.

"Kasper Meier" felt secure enough from French persecution to perform the solo part of his Piano Concerto, op. 7, under his real name—Friedrich Kuhlau—at its premiere at the Royal Theater on 23 January 1811. Of this first public appearance in Copenhagen, which was made possible by the theater's board of directors, we have an eyewitness account, which stands as one of the few contemporary descriptions of Kuhlau as a performing artist:

> On 23 January 1811, he [Kuhlau] gave a recital at the King's Theater in Copenhagen. One knew practically nothing about this foreign artist, who wanted to appear in public. The rumor had it that he was a refugee who, fleeing his homeland, had come to Copenhagen, but his arrival here was not heralded by prior fame in Europe. The curtain rose, and a slim young man appeared; his bony figure seemed to be somewhat stiff in his dark suit; he had strong curly hair and a long, ruddy face, which was disfigured by a missing eye; but otherwise he gave the impression of great openness that was contrasted by an almost childish awkwardness in his movements; one missed a certain harmony in his external demeanor. Then he sat down at the piano; Capellmeister Kunze raised his baton, and the music, a Piano Concerto in C major, commenced. At this moment all awkwardness disappeared. He proved himself a master as the sounds were produced by his hands and fingers which moved with extraordinary agility over the keys. As he rose from the piano after the last Allegro, the Danish public celebrated Friedrich Kuhlau's first appearance with applause.[2]

Even though the concert was very successful, and Capellmeister Kunze spoke positively about him, Kuhlau's application on February 27 for the position of a piano teacher at the Theater was unsuccessful. Another pianist, one Johann Christian Förster (17?-1830) was preferred. Further recitals were arranged on the recommendation of Oberhofmarschall Adam Wilhelm Hauch (1755-1838), including one at court in the Queen's apartments on 14 December 1811. On 20 February 1812, by royal resolution, Kuhlau was appointed a court musician without remuneration until a paid position might become free.[3] Still, he decided to stay in Copenhagen, perhaps because he found a friendly acceptance among the artists of the city.

Kuhlau was a frequent guest at "Sophienholm," the country estate whose owner, the merchant Constantin Brun (1746-1838), his pianist wife Friederike (1765-1835), and their daughter Adeleide (1792-1857) regularly organized so-called "Clubkonzerte" (club concerts). Introduced perhaps by his housemate Ohlenschläger, Kuhlau made the acquaintance of two local musicians, with whom his relationship later developed

---

[2] Quoted in Georg St. Bricka, foreword to *Musik til William Shakespeare: Romantisk skuespil af C. J. Boye, op. 74*, Samfundet til udgivelse af dansk musik, ser. 1, no. 3 (Copenhagen: Samfundet til udgivelse af dansk music, 1873).

[3] Graupner, 27.

in rather different ways. Christoph Ernst Friedrich Weyse (1774-1842), who had made a name for himself as a composer of religious cantatas and as a pianist, became his lifelong friend. Kuhlau wrote to Gottfried Cristoph Härtel "He [Weyse] is the greatest pianist I have ever heard, and anyone who has ever had the good fortune to hear him play his improvisations will agree that I am not exaggerating."[4] Kuhlau dedicated his Piano Concerto, op. 7, to him. Claus Nielse Schall (1757-1835), on the other hand, became a severe critic of Kuhlau's music. Schall had worked there as a composer, and after 1817 he held the position of Capellmeister of the Royal Orchestra, and in this capacity he was responsible for directing many performances of Kuhlau's operas at the Theater. The animosity was mutual. About Schall's music, Kuhlau once said "He can't put eight measures together in proper sequence."[5]

During this time Kuhlau earned his living from honoraria for his concerts, as well as from the sale of his compositions to the music publisher Härtel, who since 1810, on the recommendation of Schwencke, had published some of his pieces. "Would you be interested in publishing some of my duos for flute?" Kuhlau inquired of Härtel on 12 November 1812. Following this proposal he wrote the *3 Duos concertantes für 2 Flöten,* op. 10, dedicated to G. D. de Lorichs. Kuhlau sent them with the following letter to Härtel on 4 March 4 1813: "Dear Sir! I again take the liberty of sending you four of my pieces: German songs; flute duos—which I mentioned to you earlier; canzonettes; and a sonata." In the same letter he also commented upon the degree of difficulty of the duos: "The flute duos aren't exactly of the easy sort, but they are still playable." These remarks are still valid today. The 3 Flute Duos are especially attractive because of their skillful technique of composition which is demonstrated in the thematic development, style of the chromatic harmony, and contrapuntal implementation. In the Allegro con espressione first movement of the three-movement Duo, op. 10, no. 1, Kuhlau develops the first theme from a simple two-measure motive accompanied by the chromatic melody-line of the second flute (ex. 3.1). The same opening motive is also used for key modulation. It is also the basis for the coda through a change of direction. Kuhlau crowns the closing movement of the two-movement Duo, op. 10, no. 3, with a fugato, skillfully developed within the limited possibilities of both flutes (ex. 3-2).

EXAMPLE 3.1. Flute Duo, op. 10, no. 2, movement 1:

a. Theme 1, meas. 1-9.

Continued

[4] Letter to Härtel, 8 December 1811, in Busk, 41-42.

[5] Quoted in Adam Oehlenschläger, *Lebenserinnerungen* (Munich: G. Müller, 1923), 4:40.

EXAMPLE 3.1.–*Continued*

b. Key modulation, meas. 26-31.

c. Coda, meas. 171-75.

EXAMPLE 3.2. Flute Duo, op. 10, no. 3, movement 2, fugato, meas. 78-88.

Kuhlau who, by the way, was really hard up for money, did not receive any payment for these duos but just some sheet music from the publisher. Only for his next compositions for flute, *3 Grand Trios concertants für 3 Flöten,* op. 13, together with his *Klaviervariationen,* op. 12 and op. 15, did he receive ten *louis d'or*—and even that only after two reminders. Kuhlau sent these works to Härtel on 20 July 1814, and on that November 12 he inquired if they had been received:

> Dear Sir! Three or four months ago I sent you a letter, together with three manuscripts—*Trios für drei Flöten* and two *Themata mit Variationen für Fortepiano*—but as yet I haven't received any reply.

When he still did not get an answer, he sent a reminder again on August 12, this time in what was for Kuhlau a rather unfriendly manner: "Should you not be willing to pay me ten *louis d'or* and several free copies for these compositions, then I'll have to ask you to return my manuscripts to me with the first mail." This reminder hit the mark, and the Trios, op. 13, were published after all by Härtel in 1815. At Kuhlau's request, in a letter of November 11, "I should like to request that you delete the dedication of the title page of the Flötentrios . . .," the original dedication was not printed in the first edition.

The most demanding piece of the *3 Grand Trios concertants,* op. 13, is the Trio, op. 13, no. 1, in three movements, which is opened by a slow D-minor Adagio introduction (ex. 3.3). Within the span of an octave and also in rhythmic unison, the three flutes present a motive for which the key is still undecided. The upbeat of this motive is used by Kuhlau to introduce the two main themes of the following D-major Allegros, and thereby in this fashion he creates a direct thematic coherence.

EXAMPLE 3.3. Grand Trio concertant, op. 13, no. 1, movement 1:

a. Adagio, introduction, meas. 1-4.

b. Allegro, theme 1, meas. 25-27.

c. Allegro, theme 2, meas. 56-58.

In the Trio, op. 13, no. 3, there is also a final movement, the F-major Minuetto, with a tempo indication of Allegro assai (ex. 3.4). This movement, which is to be played in fast, one-beat measures, was the first of a whole series of scherzos that Kuhlau worked into his chamber music for flute. The contrasting middle part of the trio of this Minuetto, which is presented in A-B-A form with a coda, begins in minor and is related thematically to the beginning of the Minuetto. The third flute plays the beginning motive an octave under the other two flutes, which play sustained notes in a higher register.

EXAMPLE 3.4. Grand Trio concertant, op. 13, no. 3, last movement:

a. Minuetto, beginning, meas. 1-4.

b. Trio, beginning, meas. 1-4.

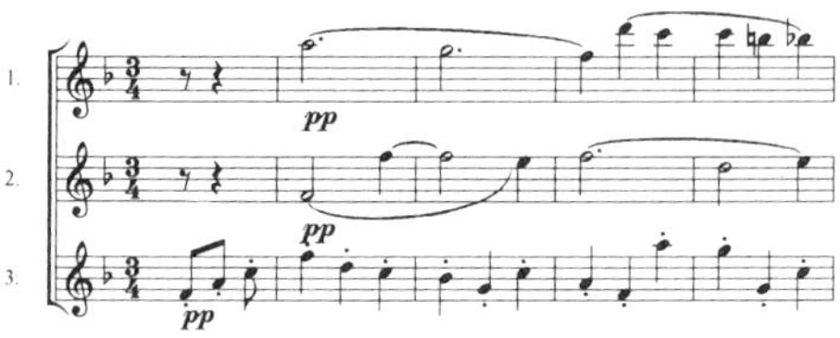

Despite his first success in selling his compositions to Härtel, Kuhlau's economic situation remained critical. In the meantime he had decided to stay in Denmark, and on 3 March 1813 he became a naturalized citizen. Soon his parents, together with his youngest sister Christine Magdalena (1793-1862), left Hamburg to join him, since the economic hardships under the French army's occupation had become unendurable. They arrived in Copenhagen in 1814, adding further to Kuhlau's difficulties since now he had to take care not only of himself but of a family of four.

This is also the time of Kuhlau's first success as an opera composer. On 26 May 1814 the premiere of his first surviving opera, *Røverborgen* (The Robbers' Fort), took place in the Royal Theater with great success. By 1879 this precursor of romantic opera had been performed ninety-one times in Copenhagen. New performances also took place in Hamburg, Kassel, Leipzig, and Riga. The libretto was written by his friend Oehlenschläger, who combined a troubadour story in the style of the French *Rettungsoper* (rescue opera)[6] with enthusiasm for nature, courtly glamor, and passions for freedom—a story very much in the taste of the times. Kuhlau wrote the music in four months at the estate of Baron Carl Løvenskiold (1783-1831), who was a supporter of the arts and had an especially high opinion of Kuhlau's music.

[6] "Rescue opera" refers to an opera where the central plot is to rescue one of the principal characters from a dangerous situation. It was a popular plot during the French Revolution. Beethoven's *Fidelio* is a well-known example, but others were written by Cherubini and Smetana. —Ed.

ADAM OEHLENSCHLÄGER
Kuhlau's friend and librettist

The grateful Kuhlau later dedicated his Flute Sonata, op. 64, to Løvenskiold's wife, Frau Frederikke Elisabeth Conradine (1787-1874).

In order to obtain more income, Kuhlau embarked on two concert tours in 1815 and 1816. The first one took him, along with the horn player Johann Cristoph Schuncke (1791-?)[7] to Stockholm, where he gave two recitals of his own compositions on 13 and 29 April 1815. A critic noted that he was a "gifted and exacting artist."[8] On the second tour he went to Hamburg, which was newly liberated after Napoleon's defeat at Waterloo. He presented two recitals on 6 March and 13 April 1816, in which he performed works of Mozart, Spohr, and his own compositions. In between these two dates, on March 22, he himself directed the Hamburg premiere of his opera *Røverborgen.*

On his return to Copenhagen, a position finally opened up at the Theater. Kuhlau became a voice teacher with a yearly salary of 500 *rigsdalers,* but he remained in this position only until 26 July 1817, when he requested his release because "teaching affairs" distracted him too much from composing. In a letter to the Theater directors, he explained:

> For a long time now I have been trying to free myself as much as possible from teaching so that I can devote my time without distractions to composing, because I soon realized how much the one [occupation] interferes with the other. I find teaching voice especially difficult, not only because of this, but also mainly because I clearly notice that my health suffers from it, since my weak chest can not bear the stress created by constantly singing demonstrations for beginners.[9]

In order to keep his salary he offered to write a new opera every year for the Royal Theater, but his proposal was not accepted. Only in 1818, after the death of Kammermusikus

[7] MGG, 12:326.

[8] Graupner, 29.

[9] Letter to the Hohe Direction des Königlichen Theaters, 4 June 1817, in Busk, 67.

(chamber musician) Junck, did Kuhlau receive his position by a resolution of the King dated 25 April 1818 with a yearly salary of 300 *rigsdalers*.

In the meantime, his operetta *Trylleharpen* (The magic harp) had its premiere on 30 January 1817, but it did not bring him any financial rewards. When the operetta was cancelled after its second performance, Kuhlau found himself in such serious financial trouble that he had to ask for a loan of 1,200 *rigsdalers*, which the Theater's board of directors finally granted him. He never repaid this sum.

JENS BAGGESEN
Librettist of Kuhlau's *Trylleharpen*

The fact that the operetta disappeared from the stage so fast had nothing to do with its quality, but rather with the genesis of the libretto by Jens Baggesen. "Baggesen managed to collect an amazing number of enemies through his pen wars, so that the play could not fail to produce some disturbance during the premiere, even if the subject matter was so excellent."[10] As soon as it became know that this opera was to be staged with Kuhlau's music, two people simultaneously raised objections. One was Peter Hjord, who contended that Baggesen had stolen his story and only translated it into Danish. The other person who objected to the staging was Capellmeister Kunzen, who insisted that he himself had almost completed the music for the piece because Baggesen had promised him the libretto in 1789. Concerned for his own music, Kuhlau turned against Kunzen and published two canons lambasting him. In the first he mocked Kunzen's extraordinary long nose:

"O du Nase aller Nasen! Nein, so gross ist meine nicht!"	"Oh, you nose of all noses! No, my nose is not that long!"[11]

In the second he took aim at Kunzen's dislike of the chromatic harmony style of Cherubini, which Kuhlau held in great esteem, and to add insult to injury he used one of Kunzen's melodies:

[10] Letter to F. L. Schmidt, 22 February 1817, in Busk, 61-62.

[11] Thrane, 24.

"Ach Musik von Cherubini	"Oh, the music of Cherubini
Ist doch gar zu chromatisch!	It is so very chromatic!
—Dafür lob ich mir Hinzen's und Kunzen's Gesänge;	—wherefore I praise the songs of Hinzen and Kunzen:
	[Everybody that doesn't count]
die sind ja wie Wasser so klar."	Since they are clear like water."[12]

The dispute came to an end only two days before the premiere of the opera because of the tragic death of Kunze who, after a contentious argument with Baggesen, died of a stroke.

In honor of the King's birthday, the premiere of *Trylleharpen* took place without any disturbance, but Kunzen and Hjord's associates conspired to disrupt the second performance by distributing in the foyer free copies of the alleged original text. There were catcalls, such as "Long live Baggesen!" followed by "Long live the real author!" and "For Kuhlau," etc.[13] After a half an hour of disturbance, the city commandant had to restore order. Because of these controversies, *Trylleharpen* was dropped from the theater's repertory. A trial followed to determine the authorship of the text, which Baggesen won, but this verdict did not bring about a repeat performance of *Trylleharpen.* The handwritten score is still in the Royal Library in Copenhagen.

The first composition Kuhlau had to write to justify the salary of 300 *rigsdalers* in his contract as Cammermusikus brought him neither success nor monetary rewards. *Elisa eller Venskab og Kjaerlighed* (Elisa, or Friendship and Love), composed for the libretto of the seminary teacher Caspar Johannes Boye (1791-1853), after its premiere on 17 April 1820 had only three more performances. The libretto of this lyrical drama, set in the milieu of the Crusades, was an "undramatic piece written by an ignorant debutante of the theater."[14]

Even if *Elisa* vanished after three performances, there were three smaller works written during the year of 1820 which, very much like his flute compositions, would make Kuhlau immortal even until today. The *3 Sonatinen für Klavier,* op. 20, have been published again and again since their first printing by Härtel in 1820 and are essential pieces in any collection of sonatinas.[15] In contemporary piano instruction, the third movement of Sonatina, op. 20, no. 1, Rondo: Allegro, continues to be one of the first classical works which can be mastered by an advanced beginner.

Later Kuhlau wrote three additional cycles of easy piano sonatinas[16] which have earned him the nickname of "Sonatinen-Kuhlau" among pianists. The prejudices

---

[12] Ibid., 25.

[13] Ibid., 28.

[14] Busk, 415.

[15] New editions: Edition Peters, nos. 715a and 715b (1900, 1989).

[16] Op. 46, op. 55, op. 88.

resulting from projecting back some conclusions based upon these piano sonatinas to his other works, and especially to his works for piano, are the reason for the refusal of many pianists to perform his larger sonatas and the variations for piano and flute.

By selling these piano sonatinas and some other compositions to Härtel, Kuhlau tried to increase his meager yearly income so that he could provide for his parents and his sister. The fact that Kuhlau, in these times of hardship, did not write any flute music which Härtel would surely have liked to publish, disproves Thrane's statement that Kuhlau's flute music was written only for money: "Kuhlau had to compose for the flute, whether he liked it or not."[17] Kuhlau took up composition for the flute again only after his first major cultural journey, from which he came back with new ideas and impressions.

---

[17] Thrane, 50.

4

First Trip to Vienna, 1821: Fantasias, op. 38

A royal resolution of 20 February 1821 granted Kuhlau's request to retain his present salary while undertaking a two-year cultural journey. Following the two earlier short concert tours to Sweden in 1813 and Hamburg in 1816, this first long trip took him to Leipzig, Vienna, and also perhaps to Munich between March and December 1821.

In Leipzig he made the personal acquaintance of his publisher of many years, Gottfried Christoph Härtel, who met him amiably. Kuhlau later, on 27 August 1821, wrote to him "Your Excellency! I want to thank you again for your gracious hospitality during my stay in Leipzig. The time spent with you was not only pleasant but also—in many ways—enlightening." In Leipzig he also met another music publisher, Carl Friedrich Peters (1779-1827), who in 1815 had rejected his Piano Sonata, op. posth. 127, but now was willing to publish his new works. Peters ordered the Fantasias for unaccompanied flute, which Kuhlau composed during his following four-month stay in Vienna. "I'm so bold, Your Excellency," Kuhlau wrote to him, also on August 27, "to let you know that I have finished the *3 Fantasien für eine Flöte* without accompaniment, which you ordered. They are written very much in the style that you desire: they are easy [*leicht*] and pleasing but still substantial pieces. The little work will come to some sixteen to twenty pages."

The *3 Fantasien für eine Flöte*, op. 38, belong to the most important solo pieces of Romantic flute music, and they are by no means "easy" to play, if Kuhlau was referring here to the technical difficulty of performance. The fingering and especially the technical tone demands of these fantasias render them practically unplayable for the amateur flutist. Also both Fantasias, op. 38, nos. 1 and 3, are in three movements and physically quite demanding, since the individual movements—as it is to be expected in a fantasia—are designated "attacca," and they are to be played like that as well. For the interpretation of these works—and in general for all of the flute music of Kuhlau—it is important to remember that one should understand "easy" (*leicht*) as meaning "buoyant" (*leichtgewichtig*), or as Hans-Peter Schmitz once said in a different way, "Nothing should be played too heavily."[1] Following this consideration, one sees, for example, in the opening measures of the first Fantasia a long-ranging, floating melody line which corresponds exactly to the Romantic *zeitgeist*.

These measures also show that one needs flexibility in tone, and a clear, agile fingering technique as a basic requirement to interpret these fantasias in a satisfactory manner. Further on, enrichment but also challenge is presented to the flutist through the employment of the right timbre. This mode of expression induced many composers during the Romantic period to write for the clarinet rather than the flute—since the clarinet at that time had a much greater modulating capacity—but with today's transverse flute one can excellently transpose the same mode of expression to the solo fantasias. So, for example, the long, stretched-out notes of the crescendo-diminuendo *messa di voce*[2] at the end of the second movement of the first Fantasia. Or by contrasting bright and dark at the thematic repetitions, as, for example, at the end of the first movement, which lend an additional expressive force to remind us again of the hidden magic of this music of former times.

The closing movements of op. 38 are presented as cycles of variations. While Kuhlau used in no. 2 the canzonetta "Silenzio che sento" by the Italian composer Francesco Bianchi (ca. 1752-1810) as a theme, in each of nos. 1 and 3 he used a Mozart theme from *Don Giovanni*. In no. 1 he used Zerlina's aria "Batti, batti, o bel Masetto" from the first act, and in no. 3 the well-known canzonetta from the second act "Deh vieni alla finestra," sung by Don Giovanni with mandolin obbligato.

For proper interpretation, a thorough knowledge of the arias is absolutely vital so that tempo, character, and phrasing can be borrowed from the singing voice. Breath marks must be set only where phrase marks of the Ponte librettos permit. This way one will not miss the point and will respect the character of these works or, in other words, sing the opera aria melodies on the flute.

Theobald Boehm (1794-1881) proposed a similar method in his book *Die Flöte und das Flötenspiel* (The flute and flute playing). In the chapter "Der Vortrag" (Musical Interpretation) he writes:

> The flutist must learn to sing with his flute, because only through singing the words of the text will he be directed towards the right way of interpretation, since only the words give him a clear idea of the emotions evoked by the sounds. Just as a composer is inspired by

---

[1] Hans-Peter Schmitz, *Flötenlehre*, vol. 2 (Kassel: Bärenreiter, 1955), 101.

[2] The slow change from light to dark in the time. Ed. note: *Messa di voce* refers to the *bel canto* practice of singing a crescendo then a diminuendo on a held note.

> poetry to express his feelings in tone, and to form melodies according to the laws of rhythm and declamation, so also the thoughtful instrumentalist can perceive the correct interpretation of the music of an aria or a song in its text.[3]

Besides composing, Kuhlau used his four-month stay in Vienna most of all to gather musical impressions, and he had plenty of opportunity there to do that. At this time Vienna had become the cultural capital of Europe, if not the world, for during the Congress of Vienna, held only six years before, "Europe brought [to the city] the glory of its thrones and courts, the power prestige of its nations, the peak of its political and military glory, the highest culture, and indeed the most exquisite blossoms of its elegance, beauty, art, and taste."[4] The number of theater, opera, and concert performances had increased enormously, and especially the operas of the Italian *bel canto* master Gioacchino Rossini (1792-1868) were frequently performed, so that his melodies infected the opera-going public with a veritable Rossini fever.

Kuhlau also felt exposed to the spell of this fever, as can be seen from an account of his experiences in Vienna that he wrote in a letter to Jacob Seligmann Trier, dated 22 October 1821:

> Vienna is just as cheerful and amiable as its inhabitants. Everybody seems to be living here only for pleasure and for enjoyment. Nature and art present so many various delights that one is often confused by the necessity of choice. Besides many different public places of amusement, there are five theaters that present plays every night. The two royal theaters, the so-called Burgtheater [Fortress Theater] and Kärnthnerthortheater [Kärnthner Gate Theater] are the most excellent, and most of their actors are well-known artists, some of them actor-singers such as Ziegler, Lembert, Madam Weissenthurm. Theater is indeed excellent here, and I go to plays more often than to the operas, because, unfortunately, the unclean spirit of Rossini reigns there.
>
> Madam Gruenbaum is the most prominent singer here; she is, in general, the greatest of all singers that I've ever heard. It is too bad that I have only heard her in Rossini operas, in which there is so much noise and clamor, especially in *La gazza ladra*, which is very popular here, in which not only do trumpets blare and drums thunder incessantly, but one is constantly deafened by larger and smaller drums, cymbals, triangles, etc., so that one would want to agree with the person, who after leaving such an opera and hearing the garrison's trumpets sounding taps, exclaims, "Thank God! For hearing soft music again."

---

[3] Theobald Boehm, *Die Flöte und das Flötenspiel* (Munich: J. Aibl, 1871), 21.

[4] Egon Friedell, *Kulturgeschichte der Neuzeit: Die Krisis der europaischen Seele von der schwarzen Pest bis zum Ersten Weltkrieg*, Ungekürzte Ausg. in zwei Bänden, 6th ed., vol. 2 (Munich: Deutscher Taschenbuch-Verlag, 1986), 957.

> During my stay here, they performed a Mozart opera, namely *Die Zauberflöte*, only once. The theater was empty, and the audience applauded only when the singers distorted Mozart's precious melodies with Rossini's embellishments. From this it is obvious that the musical taste here nowadays isn't the best.

Reading this letter one is surprised at Kuhlau's criticism of Rossini and of his instrumentation, which actually he would adopt as his own very soon. In his following theater works it is easy to recognize the original stimulus in the frequent use of cymbals and triangle *tremoli*. Also in his next compositions the element of virtuosity is given a greater role. The extraordinary influence of Rossini's music upon Kuhlau's instrumental music can be found as well in his future compositions for flute.

Kuhlau left Vienna for Leipzig, where he visited his brother Andreas, who had become the owner of a tobacco factory. Probably Kuhlau was also present for the performance of the overture to his *Trylleharpen* at a concert in the Gewandhaus on 1 November 1821.[5] Certainly, he returned to Copenhagen in December with many new impressions.

---

[5] Busk, 47.

5

Copenhagen, 1822-23: Duos, op. 39; Quintets, op. 51

At the end of 1821-22, soon after coming back from his first long culture journey, Kuhlau wrote another work for the flute, *3 Grossen Duos für 2 Flöten*, op. 39, which he sold to his publisher, Härtel. These duos reveal Rossini's influence, for the element of virtuosity is much more obvious here than in the Duos, op. 10. So, for example, at the beginning of the first movement, Allegro assai con molto fuoco, in Duo, op. 39, no. 1, the contrapuntal accompaniment is replaced by a homophonic carpet of triplets and broken triads, which is indistinguishable from the way Rossini used accompaniments in his operas (exx. 5.1-3).

Example 5.1. Duo, op. 39, no. 1, movement 1, beginning meas. 1-10.

Kuhlau himself used the kind of manneristic embellishments that in Vienna he had shrugged off as "Rossini frills." An example is the "Wechselnotenschrauben" (exchange-note-spiral) from the same first movement. The extended melody lines in the slow movements are embellished now with frills in the manner of the Italian *bel canto* style.

EXAMPLE 5.2. Duo, op. 39, no. 1, movement 1, flute 2, meas. 33-35.

EXAMPLE 5.3. Duo, op. 39, no. 1, movement 2, meas. 26-27.

Despite the virtuoso veneer, the flute parts are still written skillfully, and with proper performance they offer an enjoyable experience both for the expert flutist as well as for an audience which enjoys such a style. The growing popularity of Kuhlau's flute music can be attributed to this virtuosity, which, during the last century, a time of itinerant virtuoso players, became an important element of these performances. But despite this virtuosity, the contrapuntal and polyphonic work, the so-called intelligent style, is always present in Kuhlau's duos. In Duo, op. 39, no. 3, in four movements, there is a Scherzo third movement in which the strictest of all contrapuntal forms, the canon, is used (ex. 5.4). The movement, Allegro assai, is structured in whole measures, and consists of a hammering G-minor staccato part, a contrasting melodious G-major trio middle part, the usual *da capo* repetition of the first part, and a coda in which the major motives of both parts, but now both together in G minor, sound once again like an aphorism. In order to strengthen the contrast of the two different parts, they are designated respectively *con fuoco* and *dolce*. Throughout the whole movement both flutists play the same notes an octave apart, the second flute delayed by two measures. The first flute begins in the higher third octave, and then it pauses for four measures before the transition to the trio, to give precedence to the second flute, which plays here in the softer first octave. Before the *da capo* repetition, the second flute plays two added measures, from which the upbeat triplet is taken over by the first flute, and thus this really jocose piece starts again from the beginning. The coda ends finally with a three-measure-long *g´´* of the first flute, during which time the second flute plays its two delayed measures just to finish on a conciliatory *g´*, an octave lower.

This canon belongs to a whole series of similar pieces which made Kuhlau's name famous during his lifetime. Some of these smaller pieces composed in the manner of riddle canons were published in *Allgemeine musikalische Zeitung*. However, only one voice was published, and the reader had to find the insertion points for the other voices. The "cracking" of these riddle canons became rather fashionable, especially when composers using popular sayings with a musical bite gave them an appropriate slant. Mozart's canon for four voices "Oh, du eselhafter Peierl"

EXAMPLE 5.4. Duo, op. 39, no. 3, movement 3, canon.

Continued

EXAMPLE 5.4.—*Continued*

(Oh, you blockhead Peierl), K. 580, in which he ridiculed the Munich tenor Peierl,[1] belongs to the same category as does Kuhlau's on Kunzen. While Beethoven was later to greet Kuhlau with his "Ach, der grosser Kanonier" (Oh, the great canonist),[2] Mozart's son Franz Xavier Mozart (1791-1844) was rather against this kind of musical amusement. He wrote in his diary after a visit with Kuhlau:

> He [Kuhlau] is very found of musical artistry, which indeed, if it is nothing but that, misses the real calling of musical art. He has been busying himself with all sort of riddle-canons, and has composed a whole bunch of them, and he has invented new ways of writing them.[3]

Kuhlau dedicated his duos to the flutist Anton Bernhard Fürstenau (1792-1852), who was born in Münster, and who after 1820 held the honorable position of Royal Chamber Musician in Sachsen and was also a member of the Royal Orchestra of Dresden. Kuhlau probably met him on his way to Vienna. Later Fürstenau visited Kuhlau in Copenhagen on two occasions, in 1823 and at the end of 1829-30, which suggests a friendly relationship between these two musicians.

---

[1] Bernard Paumgartner, *Mozart*, 8th ed. (Zurich: Atlantis, 1980), 329.

[2] Thrane, 24. This was a pun on the words *kanone*—gun, and *canon*—canon. —Ed.

[3] F. X. Mozart, *Tagebuch* entry for 3 September 1819, after Kuhlau's visit.

ANTON BERNHARD FÜRSTENAU
Kuhlau's friend to whom he
dedicated his duos, op. 39

This relationship is of specially interest today because Fürstenau in his *Flotenschule* (Flute method), op. 42, of 1826, and in his major work *Die Kunst des Flotenspieles* (The art of flute playing), op. 138, of 1846, presents important guidance concerning the manner of performance of Romantic flute music, including Kuhlau's. In this respect we must also mention Hans-Peter Schmitz's 1988 book *Fürstenau heute* (Fürstenau today), in which he summarizes both Fürstenau's publications and translates the most important points into contemporary expressions. Many of these points about tempo, breathing, and articulation can be applied to Kuhlau's work and will help the contemporary player to get closer to the Romantic aspects of these compositions.

The Duos, op. 39 are the last compositions published by Härtel, who had been Kuhlau's publisher for many years. Kuhlau had to remind him twice to send his fee. The first time was on 18 June 1822, when he wrote "And you would oblige me very much if you would send me at the same time the fee for these three works, as well as for the 3 Flute Duos." On September 28 he wrote for the second time "Your Excellency must excuse me for repeating my request to send me the fee for the 3 Flute Duos, which were published a long time ago." Kuhlau was so unhappy with the compensation he finally received that he demanded the return of some new manuscripts he had just submitted, and never again signed a contract with Härtel. The next month, October 15, he wrote " I am in receipt of Your Excellency's latest letter and the very meager payment for my 3 Duos, and I have nothing further to say except to request that you send back to me immediately by return mail my three manuscripts, op. 43, 44, and 45."

The opus 45 which Kuhlau demanded returned was *Concertino für 2 Waldhörner mit Orchester* (Concertino for 2 horns with orchestra), which he had written for Johann Gottfried Schuncke, Sr. (1742-1807) and his five sons, all of whom were excellent horn players and friends of Kuhlau. This concertino—similar in character to Mozart's Divertimento—is in five movements, which, along with the double concerto of Reinhold Glière (1875-1956), in similar instrumentation, and the concert piece for four horns and orchestra by Robert Schumann (1810-56), belongs to those rare works in which the horn—in multiple instrumentation—is used as a solo instrument. About the genesis of this work there is an account concerning an incident which supposedly took place in the house of Kuhlau's friend and neighbor, the poet Frederik Høgh-Guldberg (1771-1852):

> One evening a curious improvisation took place. Kuhlau had brought along with him several of the Schuncke brothers, who were all excellent and well-known hunting horn players, and they improvised a performance with piano and hunting horn. The piano presented the theme; it was followed by a fantasia in which sometimes the piano and sometimes the hunting horns carried the main voice. The whole street in front of the house was full of ecstatic people, who, listening ardently, remained completely silent during the concert.[4]

Among the guests at these regular Friday gatherings were two brothers, Leopold and Anton Keyper. Both brothers were artillery lieutenants, but Anton Paul Wilhelm Nicolai Keyper (1796-1861) was also a piano student of Kuhlau. Flutists can be grateful to him for the adaptation of the *Trois Grandes Sonates für Flöte und Klavier*, op. 51, which he undertook in 1828 based upon Kuhlau's original score of 1822. The adapted version for flute and piano is more popular today than the original, mainly because of the instrumentation of the original, *3 Quintette für Flöte, Violine, 2 Bratschen und Violoncello,* op. 51. This instrumentation, which at first glance appears to be a classical string quintet with flute instead of the first violin, turns out to be on closer scrutiny a composition in concertante style for flute and string quartet. Similar to

---

[4] Thrane, 62.

the clarinet quintets of Mozart and Carl Maria von Weber (1786-1826), these flute quintets are really concertos for wind instruments and string orchestra in miniature, except that Kuhlau's instrumentation provides for two violas instead of a second violin. Through this a balance is created between the higher voices (flute and violin) and the middle voices (two violas), which gives an especially warm tone to these pieces. All 3 Quintets, op. 51, are in four movements, and each have a performance time of more than twenty minutes. The technical and physical demands on all the players are extremely high. They are dedicated to the Danish flutist Peter Christian Bruun (1784-1852), with whom Kuhlau liked to consult when he wrote new flute compositions.[5] Bruun, as a practicing flutist, had to check the flute parts for their technical difficulty of performance and also for the accuracy of the sheet music notes before Kuhlau sent these pieces out for publication.

The Quintets, op. 51 were published in 1823 by the publishing house of Nicolaus Simrock (1751-1832), and they were advertised in *Allgemeine musikalische Zeitung* in April 1824.[6] After the Piano Quartet, op. 50, the Quintets, op. 51, are the second of a long series of works by Kuhlau published by Simrock. Later Kuhlau would have his problems with Simrock as well because the fees he received were too meager. He wrote to Jacques-Hippolyte-Aristide Farrenc on 6 February 1830: "N. Simrock must be a bizarre old man; over and over he finds my prices too high and complains that my compositions are not being sold, and still he has published so many of my pieces."

---

[5] Ibid., 49.

[6] Robert M. Cammarota, notes to recording Kuhlau, *Flötenquintette*, op. 51, nos. 1-3 (CBS MK 44517).

6

Intermezzo, 1823-24: *Lulu*, or the Other *Magic Flute*

The impressions he received during his trip to Vienna had a lasting influence, not only upon Kuhlau's instrumental music but also upon his theater pieces. He processed these impressions in his next theater piece, *Lulu*, op. 65, which shows Rossini's influence in the instrumentation of the percussion as well as in the coloratura aspects of the vocal parts, while the overture, the colorful instrumental introductions, and the magnificent choral scenes point to Carl Maria von Weber's predominance. Kuhlau had an opportunity to study Weber's *Der Freischütz* in Copenhagen, where it had its first performance in Denmark on 26 April 1822 with the title *Jägerbruden*.[1]

The librettist for this new opera project was the poet Carl Christian Frederik Güntelberg (1791-1842), who followed the story "Lulu, oder die Zauberflöte" by Christoph Martin Wieland (1733-1813), taken from the collection of *Dschinnistan, oder auserlesene Feen- und Geister-Märchen* (Djinnistan, or Selected Fairy Tales and Ghost Stories, vol. 3, 1779). This is the same basic text which Emanuel Schikaneder (1751-1812) and Mozart were using for *Die Zauberflöte* until 1791, when the same text material under the title *Der Fagottist, oder die Zauberzither* (The Bassoonist, or the Magic Zither), with music by Wenzel Müller (1767-1835), was successfully produced in Vienna. Even though the beginning of their *Magic Flute* was already complete, Mozart and Schikaneder still had to make changes in the rest of the parts to avoid similarities with the successful competing work by Müller. This was the only reason why the Queen of the Night, an anxious mother figure, had to turn into a power hungry Fury, while Sarastro had to be transformed from a gatekeeper of Hell into a protagonist of noble Free Mason rituals. Because of such features of its genesis, many attempts to press the story of Mozart's *Magic Flute* into some sort of logical context appear to be highly amusing curiosities.

---

[1] Graupner, 39.

Kuhlau knew both the Müller version, which he had seen in Braunschweig and in Hamburg, as well as Mozart's version, through a performance he had seen in Vienna.[2] When, on 28 January 1823, he received Güntelberg's libretto from Oberhofmarschall (Lord Marshall) A. W. Hauch, Kuhlau requested in several petitions—first a raise, and then, in a letter of February 5, an advance payment of two years of his salary:

> Since despite all my strenuous efforts, I wasn't able to save enough to keep myself going during the time of composing this opera, I take the liberty of appealing once again most humbly to Your Excellency's generosity to provide me with an advance payment of my salary of 600 Rd. The composition will not be successful, if I have to struggle bitterly in order to make a living.

Such passages from Kuhlau's letters indicate his difficult financial situation, which regularly forced him to sell his compositions to publishers in order to supplement his yearly income of 300 *rigsdalers*. Hauch, who frequently supported Kuhlau and who showed a great understanding for his situation, succeeded at least partially in enabling him to receive the requested advance.

Although Kuhlau started working on the composition of his *Lulu* immediately, the planned time frame of half a year turned into a year and a half, which was interrupted only once by a two-month trip to Hamburg. Kuhlau visited there his sister Amalie and her sick husband, the businessman Nis Jepsen (b. ca. 1770), who died on 25 June 1823. The work on *Lulu* was protracted because Kuhlau used the opportunity to discuss and change minute details of the libretto with Güntelberg. He had realized that his previous operas, *Trylleharpen* and *Elisa*, had been denied lasting success because the music and text of each was not bounded together into one whole. Güntelberg originally wanted to have Weyse as his composer, but since Weyse did not like the libretto, he finally accepted Kuhlau's critical commentaries. Their intensive exchange of ideas had a positive effect upon *Lulu*. Thus a magical opera was created, which in its lyrical arias and huge choral scenes can be considered an important contribution to the Romantic operas of the first half of the nineteenth century.

The premiere of *Lulu* took place with great success on 29 October 1824 at the Queen's birthday celebration in the Royal Theater. Later performances were also favorably received. The rumor that *Lulu* was nothing but a "Rossiniada" and therefore had to be booed out of the theater, was not shared by the audience, and rightly so. *Lulu* remained in the theater repertory for thirty-two performances until 1838 when the first Sidi (the heroine of the opera), Eleonora Zrza, gave up her role, and no appropriate replacement could be found for her. Even today it is difficult to find a suitable performer for the highly demanding part of Kuhlau's Pamina. The gratifying role is written for a rare voice of a lyrical coloratura soprano who has by the beginning of the third act still to master two consecutive arias of unimaginable technical difficulty.

---

[2] Letter to Jacob Seligmann Trier, 22 September 1821.

TITLE-PAGE OF KUHLAU'S OPERA *LULU*, PIANO SCORE OF 1825

Flutists would appreciate a revival of *Lulu* because Kuhlau wrote for Lulu, the Tamino of his opera, many melodious and virtuostic solos for the flute, a feature which was highly appreciated by Güntelberg, who was himself an amateur flutist.[3] The scenes where Kuhlau has given solos to the flute are especially emphasized in the following description of *Lulu*'s plot:

In the first act of the opera Lulu receives a ring and a magic flute from Periferime, Sidi's mother; in the second act he sets out to free Sidi from the castle of the evil magician, Dilfeng. By using the power of his magic ring Lulu turns himself into an old man and forces his way into the dark dungeon of Dilfend's castle by the music of his flute (ex. 6.1). Lulu meets here the imprisoned Sidi and by magic flute music evokes in her memories of her childhood and a hope for liberation (ex. 6.2). Before Dilfeng and his spirits arrive, Lulu reveals himself to Sidi and gains her love. In a scene from the finale of the second act, which is reminiscent of the Moorish slave scene in Mozart's *Magic Flute*, Lulu barely escapes Dilfeng's spirits by bewitching them with his flute music (ex. 6.3). For the time being Sidi must stay behind in Dilfeng's castle. In the third act Lulu returns to Dilfeng's castle and frees Sidi by making everyone present fall asleep through his flute music (ex. 6.3). Finally, after further magical complications Lulu happily embraces his beloved Sidi (ex. 6.4).

---

[3] Busk, 52.

Example 6.1. Kuhlau, *Lulu*, "Flute Music in the Distance," Lulu's fantasy in his disguise as an old man as he sets out on the road to Dilfeng's castle.

Fl.

Example 6.2. Kuhlau, *Lulu*, "Süsser Klang! Süsser Zauberklang, o wie laben strömst du in die Seele!" (Oh, you sweet sound, sweet magic sound, how soothingly you enter my soul!)—Lulu finds Sidi in Dilfeng's enchanted castle.

Fl.

Fl.

Fl.

Sidi

Fl.

EXAMPLE 6.2.—*Continued*

Continued

Example 6.2.—*Continued*

Example 6.3. Kuhlau, *Lulu*, "Alle dustern Wolken weichen und es schwinden Zorn und Groll" (The dark clouds disperse, anger and hatred disappear)—Lulu bewitches Dilfeng's spirits.

Fl.

Orch.

EXAMPLE 6.3.—*Continued*

EXAMPLE 6.4. Kuhlau, *Lulu*, "Habe Dank, liebe Flöte! Alles ist nun Schlummer!" (Thank you, dear flute! Everything is but a dream!)—the beginning of the scene in which Lulu makes everyone fall asleep.

The complete recording of *Lulu* under the direction of Michael Schönwandt by the Danish Radio in 1986 to celebrate the bicentennial birthday of the composer must be considered a happy event, especially for *aficionados* of the flute. But a modern staged performance has still to come.

7

Copenhagen, 1823-25: Grands Solos, op. 67; Variations, op. 63; Sonata, op. 64; Divertissements, op. 68; Sonatas, op. 69 and 71

The work on *Lulu,* which dragged on for a year and a half, occupied Kuhlau so intensively that during this time he could write and sell to publishers only a few smaller compositions. As a result the advance he received for the planned period of six months was used up rather quickly. Immediately after the successful premiere of *Lulu*, Kuhlau appealed again in several letters to Oberhofmarschall Hauch, and his words indicate his desperate situation:

> I beg your Excellency's indulgence when respectfully I am repeating my request that you grant me a gratuity. My present situation is so desperate, I am so lacking in money (I could not earn any money for more than a year because of my work on my new opera) that I should face the greatest predicament if your Excellency would not be gracious enough to help me soon.[1]

Whereupon he was granted a one time stipend of 300 *rigsdalers*.[2] Since he had been asking for 1,000 *rigsdalers*, this amount appeared too little to Kuhlau, and therefore he applied for a position as a composer at the Theater which would have doubled his yearly income to 600 *rigsdalers*.[3] The directors of the Theater forwarded this application with a recommendation to the King. In the recommendation they wrote in part: "Kuhlau is an imaginative and talented composer of operas, whose work is appreciated both here and abroad, and his latest composition *Lulu* has been eminently

---

[1] Letter to Hauch, 5 November 1824, in Busk, *Kuhlau Breve*, 100.

[2] Ibid., 100.

[3] Letter to the Theater Directors, 7 December 1824, in ibid., 102.

recognized and honored with rare success."[4] Despite this recommendation, the King's resolution of 27 September 1825 did not offer the job to Kuhlau, but promised him an additional grant for more compositions:

> We are pleased to invite Chamber Musician Kuhlau to present a proposal for any composition of an opera or operetta for which the appropriate gratuity will be forthcoming provided that he does not enjoy any higher wages than at present.[5]

Even though the recognition of his achievements was very flattering for Kuhlau, it could not solve his financial problems, especially because he was looking after not only his parents and his sister, but since 1822 also one of his nephews, Georg Friedrich Kuhlau (1810-78). The nephew came to his house after his father, Kuhlau's brother David Gottfried Martin Kuhlau (1780-?), had accepted a position in Calcutta as a musician. The twelve-year-old boy made Kuhlau very happy since he devoted himself to music[6] and later in life became a professional musician. It can be assumed that Kuhlau regarded him like a son. To satisfy the financial needs of his family and of himself, between 1823 and 1825 he wrote, besides the three flute Quintets, op. 51, new flute compositions which he could easily sell to publishers.

In 1823, while he was still working on *Lulu*, he wrote first *3 Grands Solos für Flute mit Pianoforte, ad libitum,* op. 57, published by Kistner. The piano part for these solos is easy to perform, in contrast to the flute part, so that it can be played by less accomplished pianists. A performance, therefore, with a beginning pianist and an advanced flutist, as is frequently the case nowadays, is quite conceivable. As a matter of fact, the piano part can be omitted completely. These sorts of solo pieces, with *ad libitum* accompaniment, were very popular at that time, since they made possible performances in the open air or in places without a piano. All three Solos, op. 57, have three movements with the sequence of fast-slow-fast, and from the point of view of form can be described as solo sonatas. The final movement of no. 2, Allegretto, is a new cycle of variations based on a theme by Mozart. This time Kuhlau used the Minuet from the third act of *Le nozze di Figaro.*

In 1824 Kuhlau wrote *Introduction and Variationen über ein Thema aus Euryanthe, für Pianoforte und obligate Flöte,* op. 63, the best known and the most performed of his variation cycles. It is frequently and rightly mentioned together with Franz Schubert's cycle *Introduction und Variationen über "Ihr Blümlein alle,"* op. 160, written about the same time. Kuhlau's composition, published by Friedrich Hofmeister (1782-1864), is the first of his works in which piano and flute appear as equal chamber music partners. In the introduction and the six variations he makes

---

[4] Royal Resolutions of 1824, no. 103.

[5] Ibid.

[6] Letter to G. C. Härtel, 4 May 1822, in Busk, 92.

use of the tonal and technical possibilities of both instruments in such a way that the theme appears as if viewed through a kaleidoscope in a constantly new light. Kuhlau chose as a subject the first stanza of an aria from Weber's most recent opera *Euryanthe*, which had had its premiere in Vienna in 1823. In the two-stanza tenor-romance from the first act, "Unter blüh'nden Mandelbäumen" (Under the blossoming almond tree), Graf Adolar sings of the beauty and constancy of his fiancée, Euryanthe. In instrumental performance the performer should follow exactly the phrasing and text emphasis of the singing voice, so that the following connections and breathing pauses result.

Kuhlau's next opus was also a composition for flute and piano. *Grande Sonate brillante für Pianoforte und Flöte*, op. 64, was his first attempt at this sort of instrumentation in the sonata form. The work is extant in two versions—for flute and piano, and for violin and piano—and both were published by August Heinrich Cranz (1789-1870). The flute version is dedicated to Frederikke Elisabeth Conradine Kass (Mrs. Løvenskiold). Kuhlau frequently visited her estate as a guest, and in 1814 he had written his *Røverborgen* there. It is very likely that the son of the Løvenskiold family, the future pianist and composer Hermann Severin Løvenskiold (1815-70), whom Kuhlau described as a *Wunderknabe* and a "real magician" of the piano,[7] was Kuhlau's student. The violin version of op. 64 can be played by the flute just as well, with the exception of a long passage of sixteenth notes in the first movement, Allegro con energia, because it does not allow for any breathing pauses. Obviously Kuhlau must have had a violin performance in mind here, especially since he usually inserted short eighth notes which allow for breathing. A flutist can apply this method to the above mentioned unaccented sixteenth-note passage by leaving out one sixteenth of the broken triads (possibly the second one of a group of four).

The heart of the sonata is the middle movement, which for the first time in Kuhlau's flute music is an adaptation of a folk song. He used the old Danish folk song "Der strandet et Skib" (A ship ran ashore) once again in a later theater composition, *Elverhøj*, with the text "Der vanker en ridder." In the flute sonata he gives the song of Nordic character an introduction and eight diverse variations. The Introduction, presented solely by the piano in syncopated notes, is a program musical masterpiece lasting only for a few seconds and depicting a storm on the ocean which causes the ship to run ashore. The ocean has barely calmed down when the flute begins singing in its melancholic, soft, deep voice the simple *folkslied*. The distribution of the text allows for the following breath marks and slurs (which unfortunately are noted incorrectly in the new edition of the sonata). In keeping with the character of the song, it is recommended that the tempo be speeded up somewhat in the last two measures. Kuhlau brings the movement to an end with the theme of the folk song, transposed this time into a 6/8 rhythm while the piano accompaniment rises from harp-like arpeggios to a tremolo, depicting again the roaring ocean.

---

[7] Letter to C. A. Krebs, 30 March 1830, in Busk, 156-57.

It was again Cranz who published Kuhlau's next flute composition, *6 Divertissements für Flöte mit Begleitung des Pianoforte, ad lib.*, op. 68, which Kuhlau wrote in 1825. The sixth divertimento of this series is the famous one in C-sharp minor, which Hans-Peter Schmitz included in his *Flötenlehre*, and which he described as follows:

> This small creation of Romantic flute music . . . does not present a lot of technical difficulties; on the other hand, what is more difficult to reproduce is its concealed voice so alien to our age; a voice which comprises as much loveliness, nobility, elegance, joy of playing, and tonal beauty as well as childish yearning and sadly exquisite mourning.[8]

This is a valid description of this small treasure of flute literature, and one can add only one thing to it, that there are five other divertimentos in this series are still waiting to be rediscovered. The title "Divertissement" is used in the sense of the seventeenth-century French societal thinking, according to which amusement is recommended as a medicine against disease, and it was thought to have the possibility of leading men into a world of illusions.[9] One could speculate that this was Kuhlau's idea of amusement when he wrote the Divertimentos. They all have two movements, with the exception of no. 4, with three movements. The extraordinary feature of nos. 2, 3, and 6 is that Kuhlau intertwines the different movements into one, and this way comes to a very compact musical statement. The use of E-flat major, B major, and C-sharp minor, so seldom used in flute music, as well as the expansion of the scale to low *b*, indicate that Kuhlau knew very well the technical possibilities of the flute and practically presupposed the Tromlitz flute with its many keys.[10] Only using the Tromlitz flute would make it possible to play keys such as E-flat major and C-sharp minor, as well as the range reaching from low *b* to *b´´´* in a relatively clean fashion.[11] The piano accompaniment can either be played or left out in the same manner of op. 57.

In 1825 Kuhlau composed two other works for flute and piano: *Grosse Sonate für Pianoforte and Flöte*, op. 69, which was published by Johann August Böhme in Hamburg in 1826, and *Grosse Sonate für Pianoforte und obligate Flöte*, op. 71, published by Simrock in Bonn. The exact dating of both sonatas cannot be established with certainty. Based upon stylistic features we assume that op. 69 was written before op. 71 during or after Kuhlau's second Vienna trip of 1825. This assumption is also supported by the dedication of op. 71 to Joseph Sellner (1787-1843), a professor of

---

[8] Schmitz, *Flötenlehre* vol. 2 (Kassel: Bärenreiter, 1955), 101.

[9] Schneider, *Herders Musiklexikon*, 2:327.

[10] Johann Georg Tromlitz (1726-1805) devoted much of his life to the technical improvement of the flute and was the first to conceive of the idea of extending the application of the open finger-holes of the diatonic flute to the chromatic one of more recent times. —Ed.

[11] Hans-Peter Schmitz, *Fürstenau heute* (Kassel: Bärenreiter, 1988), 31.

oboe at the Conservatory in Vienna and a co-developer of the so-called ten-key Sellner oboe,[12] whom Kuhlau met for the first time during his second Vienna trip. If the three movements of the pretty G-major Sonata, op. 69, with its slow, lyrical harp-like middle movement in the mediant key of E-flat major, is characterized by Biedermeyer features mirroring Kuhlau's personal distress, the four movements of the E-minor Sonata, op. 71, demonstrate a fresh spirit which might be attributed to Kuhlau's experiences and impressions during his stay in Vienna. A comparison of the beginning of the first movements of both sonatas are indicative. In op. 69, the first movement, Allegro con gusto, begins with an eight-measure theme which already guarantees the smooth continuation of the sonata form of the major movement. On the other hand, the first movement of the op. 71 sonata, Allegro molto con energia, begins with a 6/4 measure, rather uncommon with Kuhlau, and with an introduction of twenty measures, which allows for a quite different musical development. The subsequent first theme is no longer a closed eight-measure phrase. It still reaches after four measures the semi-closing B major, then modulates with a widely swinging melody line towards the dominant of the major—parallel D major—and leads to a further development of the movement without limiting it.

Kuhlau's E-minor Sonata, op. 71, just as much as its twin composition, the more frequently played op. 85 in A minor with four movements, remains among the most significant compositions of Romantic sonatas for winds. For the combination of flute and piano, these two works fill the gap between the sonatas in four movements of Friedrich Schneider (1786-1853), op. 33 and op. 35,[13] and the "Undine" Sonata, op. 167, of Carl Reinecke (1824-1910).[14]

---

[12] *MGG* 9, col. 1795.

[13] Schneider, Sonata in G major, flute and piano, op. 33, and Sonata in E minor, op. 35, flute and piano (Kassel: Bärenreiter, 1987).

[14] Reineke, Sonata in E minor ("Undine"), op. 167, flute and piano (n.p.: Robert Forberg, 1900).

8

The Second Vienna Trip, 1825: Duos, op. 80 and 81

On June 15 Kuhlau received a grant to "travel to Germany for a half a year,"[1] and he left for Lübeck on July 1 by the steamship *Princess Wilhelmine.* Which cities he visited along the way is unknown, but he arrived in Vienna by July 27. As on his previous journey, he wanted to attend theater and concert performances of contemporary works not yet presented in Copenhagen in order to become acquainted with the latest events in the world of music, as well as to take home new inspiration for his own works. He was also hoping to meet personally his great idol, Beethoven. This desire was to be fulfilled.

Already by the beginning of August, Beethoven knew about Kuhlau's presence in Vienna, as documented by the notes of Beethoven's nephew Karl in his *Konversationsheft* for his deaf uncle: "Kuhlau is in Vienna. He is a Danish Capellmeister. He wrote the opera *Die Räuberburg*, which was successful in Denmark."[2] On September 2 the legendary meeting finally took place. Ignaz Ritter von Seyfried wrote a detailed account of it:

> Since the Royal Danish Concertmaster Kuhlau under no circumstances wanted to leave Vienna without having made the personal acquaintance of Beethoven, Herr Haslinger organized a small country party in Baden where he [Beethoven] had his summer residence. Herr Sellner[3] (a professor at the Austrian Conservatory), the Court Piano Builder Herr Conrad Graf, as well as the good friend of Beethoven Herr Holz, made up the company to honor the distinguished guest. Kuhlau had

---

[1] Graupner, 44.

[2] *Ludwig van Beethovens Konversationshefte*, ed. Karl-Heinz Köhler and Grita Herre, 9 vols. (Leipzig: VEB Deutscher Verlag für Musik, 1968-88), vol. 8, book 92, pp. 43ff.

[3] The man to whom Kuhlau dedicated his Flute Sonata, op. 71.

just arrived at the water spa of Hygieas, when he was warmly welcomed with a firm handshake from his host whom he had so desired to meet, and after a short pause, the call was issued: "Let's go out to take a walk in nature." Ahead, like a leading ram, the busy host, and behind him, following their fast marching leader with some difficulty, the urban foursome, whom to tire out was the major passion of their commanding host. They had to visit all the favorite places and not necessarily following a trodden path. Soon they had to climb up like mountain goats to the ruins of Rauenstein and Rauneck, from the height of which their entranced eyes could see to the promised land, laid out like an infinite carpet; then again the bold leader, seizing with a strong hand one of his guests, threw himself down the almost vertical slope with the speed of a reindeer in order to enjoy the anxious expressions of his followers as they were negotiating the slippery boulders. But after enduring these dangers, the guests found themselves richly compensated by a prepared lunch in the Helenethal, and the fact that the tired wanderers were the only guests there contributed greatly to the heightened pleasure of the occasion. The sparkling Sillery wine already there did more than its duty, and later it was crowned by a Johannissegen Vöslauer wine of the best vintage in Beethoven's apartment. The jovial host was in an excellent mood, which infected also his guests without going beyond the borderline of propriety. Kuhlau composed a canon improvisation on Bach's name, and Beethoven dedicated to this memorable day the following *Impromptu*, to which he added the next day the following lines to excuse a prickly little joke, in case the distinguished guest should have taken offense.

Baden, 3 September 1825

> I must admit that yesterday the champagne went to my head, and I had to experience once again things that impair rather than improve my judgment. Normally I'm pretty ready to account for [my deeds], but I must admit that I have no idea of what I wrote yesterday.
>
> Please remember me kindly. Respectfully yours,
>
> Beethoven, m.p.[4]

The "following *Impromptu*" was the canon "Kühl nicht lau, nicht lau kühl" (Cool, not luke warm, not luke warm, cool), which is a pun on Kuhlau's name, also using the musical notes "B A C H."

The *Konversationsheft* testifies to other visits on the following days[5] when Kuhlau also met Beethoven's publisher, Moritz Adolph Schlesinger (1798-1871). According to the *Konversationsheft*, Schlesinger later told Beethoven: "Kuhlau is

[4] *Ludwig van Beethovens Studien im Generalbass, Contrapunkt und Compositionslehre*, ed. Ignaz Ritter von Seyfried (Vienna: T. Haslinger, 1832), 235.

[5] *Beethovens Konversationshefte*, vol. 8, book 94, p. 89.

a talented man, isn't he! A cyclops! His one eye is close to his nose, didn't you notice? He must be quite a drinker; because he can hold his liquor quite well!"[6] These remarks of Schlesinger give us an accurate picture of the impression that Kuhlau must have made upon his contemporaries. The comparison with a cyclops came about because Kuhlau was rather tall and corpulent, and because he had lost one of his eyes due to his childhood accident. His increasing use of alcohol during this time heightened the comparison to an "unsteady, one-eyed giant," i.e., a cyclops.

From this time there are some interesting comments extant about "the flute Kuhlau," by a Beethoven admirer, the quartet violinist Karl Holz. Holtz observed that Kuhlau would receive from a music publisher "80 # antici-pando"[7] for six flute duos, and "Kuhlau would scribble 6 flute duets in 6 days; and 80 #!"[8] If these comments were made about the flute duos which were composed around this time, they can only refer to *3 Duos für 2 Flöten*, op. 80, and the *3 Duos für 2 Flöten*, op. 81, which actually were published by Simrock in 1827. From these short remarks by Holz one can make some interesting observations. For one thing, it is obvious how little a serious quartet violinist thought of the flute as an instrument in general and of flute duos in particular. For this reason he really could not understand why a publisher paid so well for Kuhlau's works for this instrumentation, which would sell very well. Furthermore, it indicates Kuhlau's quickness at work, if indeed these six Duos, op. 80 and 81, were composed "in 6 days."

Holz could not have known that Kuhlau wrote down very quickly on paper his other compositions, and not only the ones for flute. His dramatic music to *Elverhøj*, for example, was written in just a few weeks. But back to the six Duos, op. 80 and 81, they all are in three movements, but the slow middle movements with their exact or da capo repetitions do not reach the weight of his other compositions. The emphasis is rather on an essentially limitless fantasy-play, which while he was in Baden near Vienna Kuhlau used as the cornerstone of these duos. Especially remarkable in this series is the slow Adagio introduction to the C-major Duo, op. 80, no. 2, in which he created a mixture of fugato and canon. The progression in fifths of the two-measure fugato theme at the beginning of this introduction conceals at first the characteristics of any one key, but then it slides over finally to a movement in a non-accidental C-major Allegro con brio (ex. 8.1).

The days that Kuhlau spent with Beethoven and his friends in Baden and in Vienna were characterized by a relaxed atmosphere that never again returned, at least not in Beethoven's lifetime. It is amazing how well the hard-drinking guest from Denmark was accepted in these circles. Beethoven gave Kuhlau a lithograph of his picture with his handwritten dedication "To my friend Kuhlau from L. v. Beethoven."

---

[6] Ibid., 98.

[7] Ibid., 112.

[8] Ibid.

EXAMPLE 8.1. Duo, op. 80, no. 2, Adagio–Introduction, meas. 1-31.

LITHOGRAPH OF BEETHOVEN THAT HE GAVE TO
KUHLAU WITH HIS OWN HANDWRITTEN DEDICATION

Schlesinger invited Kuhlau to gatherings in the Zum Wilden Mann Hotel on September 9 and also most probably on September 11. He organized a luxurious party for a close circle of friends because Beethoven had given him permission to publish his latest string quartet in A minor, op. 132. This quartet was played on both evenings by the Schuppanzigh Quartet. On September 11 the Piano Trio, op. 97, was also performed, and as the zenith of the evening Beethoven himself performed improvisations on the piano, which his friend Sir George Smart later described in his memoirs as follows: "He played for 20 minutes in a quite unusual way, most of the time in full fortissimo, but a complete genius. He was excited to the highest degree at the end of his play."[9]

The impressions Kuhlau had brought home with him were lasting, and it is not improbable to presume that his only string quartet from 1831, also in A minor, and with an extended Adagio con espressione movement, harks back to the performances of those evening. In October Kuhlau traveled back to Lübeck through Leipzig, where he visited his brother Andreas, and reached Copenhagen on October 26 aboard the same steamship, *Princess Wilhelmine.*

Here, inspired by these experiences, he rushed back to work, the same as he had done after his first Vienna journey. If the first trip to Vienna produced *Lulu*, then this present trip helped him to compose the incidental music for *William Shakespeare* by Caspar Johannes Boye. It consisted of an overture, several elf choruses, and songs. This composition, which shows remarkable similarity to the theater work *A Midsummer Night's Dream* by Felix Mendelssohn-Bartholdy, as well as *Oberon* by Carl Maria von Weber, had its premiere on 28 March 1826. Due to its success, further performances followed by a total of seventeen by 1859.[10] The overture, the most impressive part of this work, has remained part of concert repertory until the twentieth century.

---

[9] Alexander Wheelock Thayer, *Ludwig van Beethovens Leben*, 5 vols. (1872-79; reprint, Hildesheim: G. Olms, 1970-72), 5:344.

[10] Busk, *Friedrich Kuhlau*, 60.

KUHLAU'S LANDLYST HOUSE IN LYNGBY (1986)

9

Lyngby, 1826-28: Sonatas, op. 83 and 85; Trios, op. 86; Duos, op. 87; Trio, op. 90

On 6 April 1826, a week after the premiere of *William Shakespeare*, Kuhlau moved to Lyngby, a village near Copenhagen. He lived here first in Landlyst House, Hostvej No. 7 in the Bondebeyn part of the village, which still exists today (fig. 9.1). He shared the large house with his parents—at that time his father was 78 and his mother 74—as well as with Georg Friedrich, his 16-year-old nephew who played the piano and whose education Kuhlau had taken charge of since 1822. On the other hand, he did not have to care for his youngest sister Magdalene any more since she had accepted a position as a language teacher in Aalborg in 1825.[1] In addition, a German servant girl from Bonn had been hired for the household with whom the family had the opportunity to talk in their mother tongue.[2] Despite his long stay in Denmark, Kuhlau himself never spoke, let alone wrote, Danish properly. For the few letters which he had to write in Danish, for example, the letters to the directors of the theater, he had to ask his friends for help.[3] We must also mention as other "members" of his family his most faithful friends, his dogs—first Achates and later Presto—which show his love of animals and nature. His love of nature must have been the reason for his moving out of the city to the country. Kuhlau liked to take long walks in the countryside with his dog; this was his best relaxation from work.

Not very far from Lyngby in Fiskerhuset House (Fisherhouse) lived the poet Christian Winther (1796-1876), a friend of Kuhlau, who visited him quite frequently. A letter written by Winther to K. Sidenius on 9 August 1826 provides us with a detailed description of his time with Kuhlau:

---

[1] Busk, *Kuhlau Breve,* 156.

[2] Thrane, 88.

[3] Graupner, 48.

> I visit Kuhlau every day; we talk about music, smoke our pipes and drink hot grog. He is really a splendid chap. He has been composing a number of smaller songs: a) two copy books with eight- and nine-voiced a cappella songs. The first of these books he has dedicated to the Student Association; b) a collection of songs with piano accompaniment. He played the alto part for me, and so far as one can follow a four-part song, played on the piano, with Kuhlau singing an aria in his husky voice; still I found it so extraordinarily blessed, indeed very remarkable, that I was ready to embrace him, and I'm not ashamed of that at all.

Nikolaj Bøgh, a biographer of Winther, also added:

> Winther was ten years younger than Kuhlau, but still they enjoyed each other's company in many ways, because both of them loved nature and loved to take long walks. They listened to the songs of birds and the folk songs: the "De gamle Folkeviser" [the old folk songs], which were still alive among the peasants. Both of them were greatly touched by Romanticism, chivalry, passion, and by the melody and poetry of this art which contained so much melancholy. Kuhlau's Danish was less than perfect, but on the other hand, Winther spoke German very well. Winther had a profound and delicate understanding of music, and Kuhlau was happy to listen to his stories about the old Danish oral tradition. When Winther visited him in the afternoons, Kuhlau welcomed him in a way that was friendly, upright, well-meaning, straight-forward and *gemütlich*, as was his nature, dressed in a morning coat with fine linen underneath, with a pipe in his mouth and with his dog Achates at his side. Winther also took his pipe, and the two went out and joined his parents in the garden. Coffee or beer was served, and sometimes a wine of rare quality, or, as Winther mentioned in his previous letter, grog. Kuhlau always liked a strong drink; it was one of his passions.[4]

Other documents testify to Kuhlau's enjoyment of tobacco and alcohol. It seems to have intensified during his stay in Lyngby, because he ordered a whole *oxhoft* (60 gallons) of red wine.[5] But despite his liking for alcoholic beverages, he never got to the point of dependency. There is no proof whatsoever of his having been an alcoholic.

In the description about Winther and Kuhlau, there is also mention of Kuhlau's fondness for "songs, which were still alive among the people." During the Romantic musical era the idea of collecting and using or reworking folk motives had become a real fashion going back to the growing nationalism of individual ethnic groups, which

---

[4] Nikolaj Bøgh, *Christian Winther*, quoted in Graupner, 48.

[5] Letter to D. Hashagen, 14 June 1826, in Busk, *Kuhlau Breve*, 105.

led to the hymn-like treatment of the simplest folk songs. Variation cycles based on folk songs were very popular at house and chamber music performances, so that music publishers were quite eager to buy such compositions. Typical examples of this sort of reworking of folk-song motives are Beethoven's variation cycles op. 105 and op. 107 written for piano and flute, commissioned by an English publisher in 1818. Kuhlau, who had already included such a cycle in his Flute Sonata, op. 64, did the same thing in his own flute compositions written in Lyngby, first in the *3 Grossen Sonaten für Pianoforte und obligate Flöte*, op. 83. Here, in op. 83, no. 1, instead of a slow second movement, there are a series of variations preceded by a piano introduction reworking the Swedish folksong "Sorgens Magt" (Sad girl).

The last movement of this sonata in three movements is also remarkable because it contains an insert of a two-part E-minor Allegro connected by an Adagio sostenuto. The rhythmic beginning of the E-minor Allegro theme changes into a G-major figure, presented first by the piano and then by the flute, accompanied by blocked chords and broken triads in the piano. This musical tapestry, harking back to hymns and frequently used in pianissimo choral scenes of Romantic operas, ends with a piano cadenza and a recapitulation of the Allegro part, before the movement closes in a virtuoso fashion with the redeeming G-major tonic of the sonata.

Also in the Sonata, op. 83, no. 2, with a slow introduction, and in no. 3 Kuhlau integrated similar transitions in the final movement. Both movements are actually abridged sonata rondos in the form of A-B-A-C-B, and part "C" is a simple folksong-like melody accompanied by harmonious chords, and in both cases differing strongly from the virtuoso character of these movements

CASPAR JOHANNES BOYE
Librettist of Kuhlau's opera
Hugo og Adelheid

The composition date of the Flute Sonatas, op. 83, can not be established precisely, but we do have exact information about Kuhlau's next flute pieces. In a letter of 17 February 1827 he apologized to his librettist Caspar Johannes Boye for not having been able to work on the music of his new opera, *Hugo og Adelheid* (Hugo and Adelheid), partly because his financial situation had not been clarified yet, and also because he was working on another composition which "was to be published by the Easter fair in Leipzig." This composition reached the publisher J. A. Böhme in Hamburg on time in April 1827. It was *3 Grande Trios für 3 Flöten*, op. 86, dedicated with appreciation to Oberhofmarschall Adam Wilhelm Hauch (1755-1838), who was the director of the Royal Theater from 1794 to 1798 and in 1810-11, and after 1811 the conductor of the Royal Orchestra,[6] and who had always supported Kuhlau's requests for salary raises and free time.

OBERHOFMARSCHALL ADAM WILHELM HAUCH
To whom Kuhlau dedicated his Trios, op. 86

All three Trios, op. 86, are excellent chamber music pieces. Their effect is in the balance between a rich melody full of yearning and a virtuoso, humorous play. The second and third of them are in three movements, while the first is in E minor (not in G major as the new edition by Billaudot wrongly states), and features a second movement Scherzo, in which the middle part in C major displays an unusual harmonic base (ex. 9.1).

---

[6] Ibid., 37.

EXAMPLE 9.1. Trio, op. 86, no. 1, movement 2, Scherzo, C-major trio.

In the Trio, op. 86, no. 2, there is a variation cycle on a folk song instead of a slow middle movement, as we have also seen in the op. 64 and op. 83 sonatas. In seven contrasting variations Kuhlau presents the old Swedish tune "Stige Lilles bjudning" (Stig Lille's invitation) in a constantly changing light (ex. 9.2). For the Trio in E-flat major, op. 86, no. 3, Kuhlau came up with an unusually melodious theme at the very beginning of the first movement, Allegro non troppo. A long whole note by the first flute is followed by the second and third flutes with an imitation of the upbeat's motive (ex. 9.3).

EXAMPLE 9.2. Trio, op. 86, no. 2, movement 2 theme, "Stige Lilles bjudning," meas. 1-12.

Example 9.3. Trio, op. 86, no. 3, movement 1, meas. 1-2.

Just at the time that Kuhlau had finished op. 86, he received by a Royal Resolution of 13 March 1827[7] a grant of 600 *rigsdalers* to work on Boye's opera *Hugo og Adelheid.* Since 1825 he had repeatedly postponed working on this banal love story set in a German Hanse city,[8] so that he could finish and send off to the publisher his flute trios. Only now, when the grant of two years of his salary beckoned, did he set to work in earnest, since the premiere of the opera had to take place at the celebration of the Queen's birthday on 29 October 1827. The completed score was sent to the copyists on October 13 so that there were only two weeks left for writing out the individual parts and for rehearsal. *Hugo og Adelheid* was performed altogether only five times with modest success before this last opera of Kuhlau's disappeared from the repertory. (Whether it was the dramatically unworkable libretto of Boye or the uninspired music of Kuhlau to be blamed for this will not be discussed here.)

During this period Kuhlau was more intensely concerned with his flute compositions. At the same time when the Sonatas, op. 83, and the Trios, op. 86, were composed, he also tried to sell other works to the Mainz court music publisher, B. Schott's Söhne. (This important German music publishing house had been inherited after the death of its founder Bernhard Schott, 1748-1809, by his sons Johann Andreas, 1781-1840, Johann Joseph, 1782-1855, and Adam Joseph, 1794-1840, and it still exists today as B. Schott's Söhne.) When in a letter to the publisher dated 14 October 1826 Kuhlau announced his compositions:

> 1 Piano Sonata with flute, soon
> 3 Flute Duos
> 1 Flute Trio for 3 Flutes, later

The court music publisher ordered all of these works at a price of three Dutch ducats per *bogen* (printed sheet).[9]

On 2 February 1827 Kuhlau sent first his *Grosse Sonate für Flöte und Klavier,* op. 85 to Schott, accompanied by the following letter:

---

[7] Graupner, 49.

[8] Letter to Theater Directors, 28 June 1825, in Busk, 103-04.

[9] A *bogen* was four pages of music notation.

> Herewith I am sending you that piano sonata with flute mentioned earlier, and I hope that it may be to your liking. The other works which you have ordered, I will have the pleasure to send to you by and by. I would very much appreciate your kindness to acknowledge the receipt of this manuscript.

The Sonata in A minor, op. 85, in four movements, is today the most frequently played flute sonata by Kuhlau, and along with his E-minor Sonata, op. 71, which is also in four movements, it is one of the most important compositions of Romantic flute music. With almost thirty minutes of playing time, it presents enormous physical demands on both performers. The first movement, Allegro con passione, begins with a simple eight-measure A-minor theme with a narrative content presented first by the piano alone. This theme appears again in the form of a reminiscence just before the end of the movement in the coda, introduced by a frantic chromatic ascending scale of the flute. It peters out here finally in a recitative dialog between piano and flute like a calm before the storm, introduced by the flute with a staccato run in sixteenths, slowly spiraling upwards which closes the movement with stormy virtuosity.

After a Scherzo with a contrasting trio middle part, the third movement of the sonata follows—an Adagio which lasts for 8½ minutes, this time not in a simple A-B-A form but rather in an extended main sonata movement. The first theme in this movement shows a definite similarity to the "March of the Priests" in Mozart's *Zauberflöte*, and it underscores Kuhlau's preference for using this kind of deceptive ending. A sonata-rondo, designated Allegro poco agitato, closes this ambitious composition.

On 20 April 1827 Kuhlau sent to Schott his *3 Grande Duos für 2 Flöten*, op. 87, the second work dedicated to his friend P. F. Thornam, Councilor in the State Chancellery, accompanied by the following letter:

> I am pleased to see from your recent letter of March 8 of this year, that you are thinking of publishing my sonata with flute soon. Herewith I am sending to you the 3 flute duos ordered by you in your letter of Nov. 24 of last year; I have worked very diligently on these pieces, and I think they have turned out quite well. Since I will undertake a journey soon, and after my return I will have to compose an opera for the Danish Royal Theater, I won't be able to work on the other compositions which you have ordered. For this reason, I thought you might want me to send to you first the second of the three works which you have ordered.

The *Allgemeine musikalische Zeitung* published the following review of the Duets, op. 87, which testifies to the high regard which they enjoyed at that time:

> No matter how many times this reviewer has had the opportunity to listen to the duets of this master, the compositions have brought each time the happy proof that Herr K. is a master of this difficult musical

> form. His profound knowledge of the art of double counterpoint serves him well in keeping his music interesting, even after repeated listening. His melodies are almost always beautiful, one could say sublime; the melodies of the same composition relate to each other, or they are related to each other in character, and when he departs from this [principle], it is easy to understand the reason for the change. . . . Everything is there in its right place. One is left with no unfulfilled desire, and one has the feeling that all the details are in the right sequence and thus create a whole, and this is the finest satisfaction. What has been said previously about the value of Kuhlau's flute duets here in the *Allgemeine* also holds for the present work, except that it is somewhat more gallant than were his previous compositions. The second of the duets, the G Minor, is probably going to be a favorite piece of flutists. . . .[10]

The ideas expressed in this review to a great extent are still valid today. The Duo, op. 87, no. 2, in G minor is really the most interesting piece of this series. At first it appears to have only two movements, but Kuhlau has inserted in the Presto agitato second movement an Adagio instead of a second theme, which brightens up the sober G-minor mood, first in the major parallel B-flat major in the recapitulation and then in the following G-major tonic (ex. 9.4).

Example 9.4. Duo, op. 87, no. 2, movement 2, theme 1, meas. 1-8; theme 2, meas. 95-99.

As far as the Duos, op. 87, no. 1, and op. 87, no. 3, in three movements are concerned, one has to note that Kuhlau presents here a frequent change of voice that is rich in variety for the players but appears to be just repetition for the listeners.

The third flute composition ordered by B. Schott's Söhne, *Trio für 3 Flöten*, op. 90, announced by Kuhlau in his letter of 20 April 1827, was only completed during the year of 1828. The reason for the delay was not only Kuhlau's preoccupation

[10] *Allgemeine musikalische Zeitung*, no. 47 (November 1828).

with his opera *Hugo og Adelheid*, but mainly the late and insufficient payment from the publisher in Mainz. On May 29 Kuhlau asked the publisher to be paid.

> I have received no answer to my letter of April 20 of this year with which I enclosed the three flute duos. Since I am experiencing financial difficulties, I would like to take the liberty of inquiring if I can transfer my bills to your account in an approximate amount for the two compositions sent to you—the piano sonata with flute and the three flute duets, or perhaps you may have some other way to send me the fee.

Whereupon Kuhlau received payment, however, it was less than expected according to the contract; therefore in a letter of November 3 he asked for the rest of his fee:

> Following my letter of May 29 of this year in which I requested prompt payment for my compositions of op. 85 and 87, you were kind enough to have Mr. Lose pay me 200 F. However, this is only a small portion of the honorarium still owed to me, and since I have also heard from Mr. Lose that both works have already been published, I am beseeching you to pay me the rest as soon as possible. Unfortunately I am not so well off that I can wait long for my honorarium. Therefore, in the future, I can send you further compositions only under the following conditions: you pay me 3 ducats for every sheet (and you know that I do not write very diffusely), and you pay me within three months after the receipt of my work. If this is acceptable to you, I will send you soon a Trio for 3 flutes.

Since Kuhlau did send his Trio, op. 90, to Mainz in 1828, it can be assumed that the court music publisher had paid the rest of the honorarium before delivery. But, even about the published score of op. 90 there were still some disagreements concerning misprints that had not been corrected since the first edition:

> In my work printed by you, besides the misprints already noted, the following fourth measure is missing from the *Trio* in the finale (where it turns to B major) in the score of the third flute:
>
> 3. 
>
> which will lead to a serious quarrel among the performers.[11]

In the new edition of the Trios, op. 90, published in 1981 by Schott, the misprints were corrected, so that the "performers" won't have to "quarrel" among themselves

---

[11] Letter to B. Schott's Söhne, 20 January 1829, in Busk, 120.

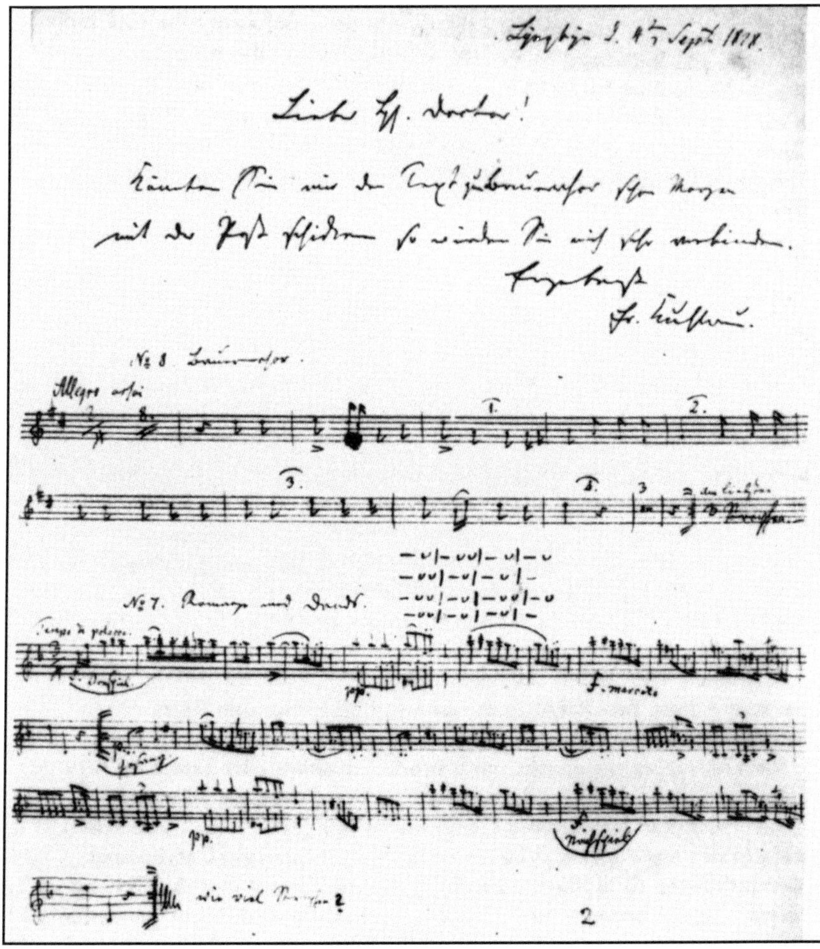

KUHLAU'S LETTER OF 4 SEPTEMBER 1828 TO JOHAN LUDVIG HEIBERG, WITH THE FOLKSONG 'NECKENS POLSKA' (HERE, NO. 7)

about them. And since this work, in four movements, is of the same high quality as the E-minor Trio, op. 86, no. 1, today one can "quarrel" only about the preference of the "performers" for one or the other of the compositions.

In 1828, the year in which he composed op. 90, Kuhlau set out on another journey which took him to Sweden and Norway between May 2 and June 5. On May 13 he gave a concert in Götenborg, where he performed his latest piano work, *Variationen über das alte schwedische Volkslied "Och Liten Karin tjente,"* op. 91. At this time he did not know that immediately after his return to Copenhagen he would be dealing rather intensively with this kind of folk tune. The wedding of Wilhelmine, the daughter

JOHAN LUDVIG HEIBERG

of Friedrich VI, and Prince Friedrich was set for 1 November 1828. To honor this event a new work was to be presented in the Royal Theater. The theater directors chose a libretto by Heiberg, *Elverhøj* (Elf Hill), which, following the example of Mendelssohn's *Midsummer Night's Dream*, was to combine drama, music, opera, and ballet. Kuhlau, as the theater composer, was commissioned to write the music, consisting of an overture and individual musical numbers. The content of the play, designed to glorify the Danish royal house, expressed the soul of the Danish people, which Kuhlau intended to support in his music by reworking old Nordic folk songs. The exchange of letters between Kuhlau and Heiberg show that Kuhlau selected old Swedish folk songs especially from the anthology entitled *P. Gronland: Alte schwedische Volksmelodien*, collected by E. G. Geijer und A. A. Afzelius.[12]

The collaboration worked the following way: Kuhlau chose the folk songs, which he sent then to Heiberg who wrote new texts for the melodies to fit the content of the play. This is why the melody of Romance no. 7, "Der vander en ridder," is identical with the Danish folk song "Der Skib," which Kuhlau especially liked and which he had already inserted into his Flute Sonata, op. 64, in 1824. Romance no. 9, "Dybt i havet," originally the Swedish "Neckens Polska," Heiberg simply translated into Danish and introduced as a narrative in the play. To this ballad about the old Germanic water spirit "Neck" or "Nöck," which Richard Wagner turned into Alberich in his *Ring des Nibelungen*, Kuhlau later dedicated a whole variation cycle in his Flute Duos, op. 102.

In all, Kuhlau instrumentalized these folk songs in *Elverhøj* so cleverly and wove them together with his own melodies so well that the legendary story from old Denmark came alive for the audience. Heiberg's text relating the story of the famous Danish King Christian IV (reigned 1588-1648), who, on the way to Højstrup, the residence of the king of the elves, to celebrate his wedding, meets with magic figures such as Mutter Karen (the Danish Erda), who in their folk songs narrate to him the history of Denmark, contributed greatly to the lasting success of this play.

In act 5—a ballet to honor the betrothed couple, in the middle of the Polonaise no. 15—there is a solo piece for flute and orchestra, which may be a small consolation for the fact that Kuhlau had not written a solo concerto for this instrument so generously used at other times. The finale of *Elverhøj* is a hymnal reworking of the

[12] Letter to Johan Ludvig Heiberg, October 1828, ibid., 119.

AN IDEALIZED DEPICTION OF HEIDBERG (ON THE LEFT) AND KUHLAU AFTER THE TRIUMPHANT PREMIERE OF *ELVERHØJ*, FROM A CONTEMPORARY POSTCARD

Danish national song "Kong Christian stod ved højen Mast" (King Christian stands at the high mast). This hymn closed the generously set potpourri overture to *Elverhøj*, resembling rather closely the 1818 *Jubel Overture,* op. 59, by Weber, which closes with the English national anthem "God Save the King."

The premiere of *Elverhøj* on 6 November 1828 was a triumph for everybody involved, and especially for Kuhlau, who during the wedding celebrations five days before the premiere was promoted to professor with a two-fold increase in his salary. *Elverhøj*, with more than one thousand performances, has remained the most successful production of the Royal Danish Theater and rendered Kuhlau immortal in Denmark as the Danish national composer of German descent. With the first Danish national song Kuhlau also laid the foundation for the next generation of Scandinavian composers, Niels W. Gade (1817-90), Johan Svendsen (1840-1911), Edvard Grieg (1843-1907), and Carl Nielsen (1865-1931), who followed this line of development in their compositions.

10

Lyngby, 1829: Variations, op. 94; Fantasias, op. 95; Introduction et Rondo, op. 98; Variations, op. 99 and 101; Duos, op. 102; Quartet, op. 103; Variations, op. 104 and 105; Duos, op. 110

At the time of the triumphal performance of *Elverhøj*, Kuhlau received a veritable flood of commissions for compositions and flute pieces. For this reason in 1828 he composed ten opus numbers with flute for different publishers, eight of which were ready by the end of April.

The first publisher to commission flute pieces was Carl Gotthelf S. Böhme (1785-1855),[1] who had taken over the Leipzig publishing house after the death of C. F. Peters in 1827 and who had written a letter to Kuhlau on 24 November 1828. Kuhlau replied to Böhme on 20 January 1829:

> I am extraordinarily happy about your desire to publish my compositions. Presently I have nothing ready for publication; however, I am in the process of writing some variations for several popular themes for flute and piano (concertizing on both instruments). Should you be interested in any of them, please let me know as soon as possible. My price is: one Dutch ducat per score page. . . .

On March 14 Kuhlau sent to Böhme three manuscripts ready for publication. He was particularly happy about Böhme's acceptance of his fee request (in view of which he raised his price for B. Schott's Söhne from three to four Dutch ducats per sheet):

> I am sending here, Your Excellency, the works offered in my first letter to your publishing house, [which are] works for flute and piano, op. 94, 98, and 99. I hope the selection of the themes taken from

[1] Not to be confused with the Hamburg publisher J. A. Böhme.

> Onslow's popular opera will meet with your approval. I am particularly happy to see from your letter of January 27 that you accept my conditions pertaining to the fee, and that in this respect we are in complete agreement. . . .

Böhme was the only publisher in Leipzig to pay the fee in full and on time. On the other hand, the publisher initially announced the three works, op. 94, op. 98, and op. 99 incorrectly, as Kuhlau complained in his letter of April 25:

> The announcement sent to me by your publishing house describes my works op. 94, 98, and 99 as "Trois Fantasies pour une Flûte." Should this not be a mistake? I believe that you can't call variations and rondos fantasies since the latter require a completely different style, and then "pour une flute"? The piano part is not ad libitum, but is just as important as that of the flute.

When Böhme made the changes, Kuhlau was happy both with the prompt payment and with the published form of his works:

> I must admit that I have never come across such elegant and correct editions as those of your company. I am sure that no other publisher has ever equalled your achievements in this field.[2]

All three works use themes from the comic opera *Le Colporteur* (The door-to-door salesman) by Georges Onslow (1784-1835), with which Kuhlau had become familiar during its performance in Copenhagen on 28 September 1828.[3]

The first of these works, *Variations concertantes über das Arie "Por des filles si gentilles" aus Le Colporteur, für Klavier und Flöte*, op. 94, consists of an eight-measure piano introduction, a theme in the original key of B-flat major, and eight variations. The piano part is a transcription of the orchestra introduction to the aria; the aria itself was used almost literally. Noteworthy is the sixth variation, in B-flat minor, an unusual key for the flute.

The second work is not a variation cycle, as described by Karl Graupner in the appendix of his dissertation, but is rather an *Introduction et Rondo concertantes über den Chor "Ah! quand il géle," aus Le Colporteur, für Piano und Flöte*, op. 98. Following a Maestoso introduction, similar to a cadenza and dominated by the piano,

---

[2] Letter to Böhme, 10 April 1830, in Busk, *Kuhlau Breve*, 158-59.

[3] Ibid., 122. Onslow was a French composer of English descent who is best known today for his numerous string quartets and quintets. His three operas are now forgotten but they were popular at the time reflecting the influence of Cherubini and Méhul. Of the three, *Le Colporteur* enjoyed the most success. First performed in Paris on 22 November 1827, within four years it had been translated into German and English and performed in Graz, Budapest, Berlin, and London. The Danish translation was done by Kuhlau's collaborator Johan Ludvig Heiberg.—Ed.

the E-minor theme is developed in a concertante sonata rondo, in which Kuhlau retains his usual key progression: minor tonic—major parallel—minor tonic—major tonic, but without contrasting the first theme with a second. The transcription of the original theme is again practically without change, even to the point that Kuhlau retains the instrumentation itself, so that the flute—in Onslow's score the piccolo—repeats the theme an octave higher.

The third work, *Introduction et Variations concertantes über die Arie "Toujours de mon jeune âge" aus Le Colporteur, für Piano und Flöte*, op. 99, begins with an A-major introduction, starting with a flute cadenza. The following A-minor theme, first introduced by the piano alone, is presented in the proven fashion, in eight variations. In variation 8, Allegro alla polacca, the virtuostic scale in the dominant key is suddenly interrupted, and again, unchanged, the first four measures of the theme appears before the flute joins the swiftly running sixteenth triplets of the piano in thematically related octave slurs in order to finish the cycle in a stormy virtuostic fashion.

In contrast to the *Introduction et Rondo*, op. 98, which is available again in a new edition by Billaudot, the other two variation cycles, op. 94 and op. 99, were only just rediscovered by the author of this work. These are the only flute pieces by Kuhlau that have not been reprinted since their first publication in 1830. For the following analysis I used copies of the first editions, which are being made accessible again the public for the first time.

ARISTIDE FARRENC
Flutist and music publisher

While he was in the midst of work on these compositions, a second publisher, Jacques-Hippolyte-Aristide Farrenc (1794-1865) wrote to Kuhlau to commission flute pieces. Farrenc, who had set up a music publishing house in Paris, was himself a flutist, a pupil of the virtuoso Joseph Guillou (1787-1853). In contrast to the pleasant cooperation with Böhme, Kuhlau experienced with Farrenc the usual difficulties: he did not pay punctually, wanted to knock down the price, and even stipulated a certain length of a composition. On 6 February 1830 Kuhlau wrote to him:

> You want me to expand my rondo by two pages. I really cannot bring myself to do this. It would amount to a patchwork, the rondo would be spoiled, and also it would disturb the work which I am presently engaged in.

From notes like this it becomes obvious what unbelievable conditions were set upon composers by publishers of that time. For Farrenc, Kuhlau wrote three opuses for flute: in March, *3 Fantasien für Flöte mit Begleitung des Pianoforte ab libitum,* op. 95,[4] and then *Introduction et Variations brillantes über ein Thema aus Jessonda für Pianoforte und Flöte,* op. 101, and *3 Duos Brillantes für 2 Flöten,* op. 102. Kuhlau sent the latter two manuscripts to Farrenc on 24 April 1829, followed by a letter written the next day in which he stated "Yesterday I sent out to you by parcel post my op. 101 and op. 102."[5]

LITHOGRAPH OF KUHLAU BY W. C. WIEHE, TO WHOM HE DEDICATED HIS *FANTASIEN,* OP. 95

Kuhlau sold the *3 Fantasien* not only to Farrenc in Paris, but also to Johan Cristopher Daniel Milde (1788-1864), a publisher in Copenhagen, whose first printing is the basis of the new edition available again today. Op. 95 is dedicated to the painter C. W. Wiehe, who was a friend of Kuhlau. In style of composition, they follow the *Divertissiments,* op. 68, and the *Grands Solos,* op. 57, with the same instrumentation. Their title "Fantasien," meaning free fantasies or improvisations in the nineteenth-century sense of the word, can be best applied to the first of these works. An Allegretto pastorale in 6/8 time, kept in the simple triads of a folk tune, is followed by a fierce Allegro assai un poco agitato in the contrasting key of G minor. Before closing the fantasia with a vividly virtuostic G-major coda, the beginning 6/8 time pastorale appears again, shortened as though "fantasizing."

[4] Letter to Farrenc, 14 March 1829, in Busk, 122-23.

[5] Letter to Farrenc, 25 April 1829, in ibid., 127-28.

The individual movements of op. 95, nos. 2 and 3, are not related thematically, but still they are connected through transitions, so that the impressions of a single and complete fantasia remains. The piano, which has nothing but a supporting harmonic function, can be left out, as in op. 57 and op. 68.

The second work written for Farrenc, *Introduction et Variations brillants über ein Thema aus Jessonda, für Pianoforte und Flöte,* op. 101, is a continuation of the *Colporteur Variationen,* op. 94 and op. 99. Flute and piano are treated as equal duo partners. The piece is dedicated to the Copenhagen flute soloist Niels Petersen. Kuhlau's theme, as Farrenc expressly requested, was not French, but German from the opera *Jessonda* by his acquaintance Ludwig Spohr, first performed in Kassel in 1823. The duet "Schönes Mädchenwirst mich hassen" (Beautiful girl, you will hate me) is from the second act. This is the scene between Nadori and Amazili whose marriage is delayed by the rescue of Jessonda, Amazili's sister, promised but not yet carried out by Nadori.

Kuhlau transposed the first sixteen measures of the duet from A-flat major to G major, which is first played by the piano alone and set for both flute and piano in the repetition. He preceded this theme with a G-minor introduction, which with its piano tremolos and rhythmically-defined motives would rather introduce a world of the opera than a chamber music variation cycle. The effect of the following eight variations lies in a presentation of brilliant virtuosity. The passages in which Kuhlau develops the theme with great artistry and latent two-voice harmony rank among the outstanding virtuoso variations of his time. On the other hand, in connection with this work, one can no longer talk of a closed variation cycle, as was the case with the *Euryanthe Variations,* op. 63.

The third work written for Farrenc, *3 Duos brillantes für 2 Flöten,* op. 102, is dedicated to Kuhlau's friend Moritz Lobel, and closes the circle of the eighteen flute duos written by Kuhlau. Particularly noteworthy is Duo no. 2, in which the closing movement is a variation cycle on the Swedish song "Neckens Polska" used already in *Elverhøj*. After the two preceding movements—an Adagio introduction in E major and a frantic Allegro assai con molto fuoco in E minor—one is left with the impression of a super dimensional introduction, which leads the audience into the crystal clear underwater world of the "Neck," the old Germanic spirit, who is celebrated in "Polska." Especially in the Allegro assai con fuoco with its E-minor triads distinguished by the "neckisch" (sweet) short-octave grace notes and the frenetic water-spewing "triplet chains," the melody moves deep down to the grotto hall at the bottom of the sea—the home of the "Neck" (ex. 10.1). As a further intensification the movement closes with a canon-like conclusion of the basic theme with a direction to the performer, *Più presto ff con molto fuoco* (ex. 10.2). Then we hear the ballade of the "Neck" in four variations and a coda in which both flutes are treated as equal, and the repetitions of the folk songs are noted by a change of the two parts (ex. 10.3). The "Tempo de polacca" direction for the ballade is misleading and refers not to the tempo but to the polonaise rhythm of the song, which in

EXAMPLE 10.1. Duo, op. 102, no. 2, movement 1, beginning of the Allegro assai con molto fuoco, meas. 28-32.

EXAMPLE 10.2. End of the above section, meas. 163-79.

EXAMPLE 10.3. Duo, op. 102, no. 2, movement 2 (Variations on an ancient Swedish air: Tempo di polacca), "Neckens Polska" theme, meas. 1-24.

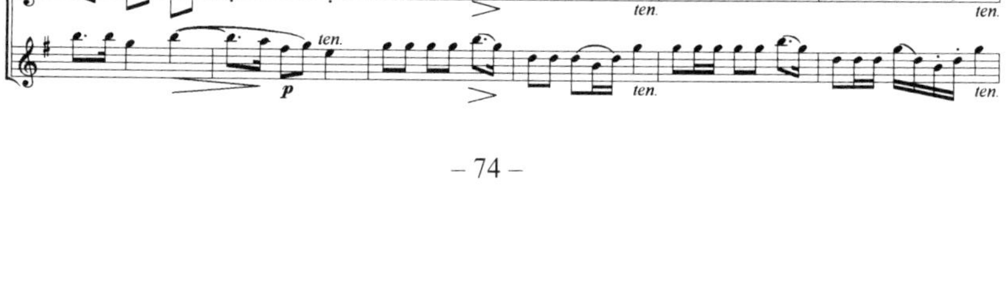

Example 10.3.—*Continued*

Swedish is a rural round dance. After a cadenza by the first flute, Kuhlau's Duo no. 2 closes with a second fast coda, in which the first measure of the song is again be interwoven with the familiar triplets from the second movement (ex. 10.4).

Example 10.4. Duo, op. 102, no. 2, movement 2, ending, meas. 147-54.

A letter written by W. L. Huntly to Kuhlau on 4 April 1829 prompted the seventh and eighth flute compositions that he finished by the end of April. This flute dilettante requested fantasias on Celtic folksongs for flute and piano *ad libitum*. Kuhlau replied to him on April 25:

> I am in receipt of Your Excellency's highly esteemed letter of the 4th of this month, which is very flattering to me, and I am extremely delighted to find that my flute compositions pleased you. I am grateful for your sending me the 2 beautiful folk songs. On the other hand I have recently published 3 solos or rather fantasias for flute (with piano accompaniment ad libitum) in Paris by Aristide Farrenc, and in Copenhagen by C. D. Milde (op. 95). Thus, as you wished, I have composed variations on these 2 themes for flute in a brilliant and melodious way with easy piano ad libitum. With your permission I

> would like to dedicate these two little pieces to you, since you have initiated their composition, and publish them this summer with some publisher either in Leipzig or in Paris.

Kuhlau kept his word and sold both manuscripts in the summer of 1829 to his Leipzig publisher Böhme,[6] which he reported immediately in a July letter to Huntly: "Well, I just sold these two little works to C. F. Peters—Bureau de Musique in Leipzig." The two "little works" are actually *Variations sur un air favori ecossais, für Flöte mit Klavier, ad lib.*, op. 104, and *Variations sur un air favori irlandais, für Flöte und mit Klavier, ad lib.*, op. 105. Both works are dedicated to Huntly.

For op. 104, Kuhlau used the Scottish folk song "Durandarte and Belerma," and for op. 105 the Irish folk song "The Last Rose of Summer," which was very popular at that time. Beethoven also made use of this Irish folk song in his Variations, op. 105, no. 4, in reversed instrumentation (piano with flute *ad lib.*).

Kuhlau's variations on two very similar folk songs in direct sequence may have something to do with the high price which Huntly surely paid for the two variation cycles. Both of these works follow the typical genre of the period—bravura variations for the flute, while the piano is merely given the function of playing the accompanying chords.

After the total of eight flute works—the three compositions for Böhme, three others for Farrenc, and two for Huntly, all written shortly one after another in April 1829—Kuhlau requested a rest for a while from flute compositions. He wrote to Farrenc on 25 April 1829:

> It is really a difficult job for me to write three flute duets two times one after another, therefore I want to find some relaxation first in some other kind of works, and later to satisfy your request, by composing 3 grande flute duos, even though I would first rather write 3 trios for 3 flutes or 3 sonatas for piano and flute.

Kuhlau rejected another request from Paris, this time by composer, piano builder, and publisher Ignaz Pleyel (1757-1831), because of existing publishing rights arrangements:

> I have the honor to reply to Your Excellency's esteemed letter that Herr Aristide Farrenc desires to be the sole publisher of my flute compositions in France, and in this respect I have entered into an agreement with him.[7]

But it was not a long pause without flute compositions after all. Already in the summer of 1829 Kuhlau's next work, *Grosse Quartett für 4 Flöten,* op. 103, was

---

[6] This publishing house is now owned by C. F. Peters.

[7] Letter to Pleyel, 28 March 1829, in Busk, 124-25.

created and dedicated to the Berlin flutist Julius Gabrielski (1806-78), whom Kuhlau had met on the first stop of his trip to Berlin and Leipzig with his friend Gerhard Diderich Hashagen (ca. 1792-1859).

Whether the Quartet, op. 103, was written shortly before or during the trip can not be established today, but in July 1829, when Kuhlau arrived in Leipzig, the second stop of his journey, the Quartet was already completed, since he had it performed for the first time at the country house of his publisher Carl Böhme in Connewitz. Thrane writes:

> During his first trip to Leipzig Kuhlau was invited by the music publisher Böhme (Peters' Bureau) who wanted to hear his new quartet for four flutes. The first flutist, talking to Kuhlau, posed some thorny technical questions concerning the flute, and he was so absolutely amazed to hear that Kuhlau was not a flutist, that he did not want to believe it.[8]

The Leipzig flutist was very likely Karl August Genser (1794-1864), who had been the solo flutist in the concert and theater orchestras since 1814, and his remark shows that Kuhlau's works written especially for the flute were very highly regarded by professional flutists. Böhme, who made here in person Kuhlau's acquaintance and with whom he established a friendly relationship, also liked the quartet. He bought the manuscript immediately, and later his company C. F. Peters published it. The Quartet, op. 103, described by Reinhold Sietz as "the best of this art,"[9] is in four movements. The first movement, Allegro assai con molto fuoco in E minor, is preceded by a slow introductory Andante maestoso in E major. The dotted rhythms lend this slow introduction the character of an overture, which closes with a cadenza by the first flute and leads on to the magnificent work itself. In all four movements of this Quartet Kuhlau

KARL AUGUST GRENSER
One of the flutists who performed Kuhlau's Quartet, op. 103, for the first time at Carl Gotthelf S. Böhme's country estate, Connewitz

[8] Thrane, 48ff.

[9] MGG, 7:1878.

demonstrates his ability to apply the four flutes in a manner normally reserved for a string quartet.

Kuhlau returned home with new impressions which were especially colored by the numerous theater productions he had seen in Berlin. He later described his stay in Berlin as "a real Paradise."[10] His visit to Leipzig was equally rewarding, for he wrote to his publisher Böhme on 4 August 1829 "My pleasant stay in Leipzig, the pleasure of having made your acquaintance, and the wonderful hours spent there together—all this appears now as a beautiful dream which I hope I can dream again." By the time this letter reached its destination, Kuhlau was back again in Copenhagen which he had reached on 31 July 1829 after a stormy crossing on the steamship *Caledonia.*[11]

JOSEPH GUILLOU

The recipient of Kuhlau's flute canons

At the end of October 1829 Kuhlau met in Copenhagen one of the most famous piano virtuosos and accompanists of his time, Ignaz Moscheles (1794-1870), who together with the soprano Pauline Anna Milder (1785-1838) and the French flute virtuoso Joseph Guillou (1787-1853) performed two much celebrated concerts on November 5 and 20. In the house of the wine merchant Christian Waagepetersen (1787-1840), who being a great sponsor of arts liked to host private concerts, Kuhlau and Moscheles had the opportunity to meet with some frequency. Moscheles was particularly enchanted with Kuhlau's incidental music to the opera *Elverhøj*, which he had enjoyed hearing at the Royal Theater, as well as with the riddle canons. He wrote in his autobiography "I met Kuhlau, the overall clever riddle canon maker; he is a smith of artistic musical locks, which are infinitely difficult to open."[12] As a going away present Kuhlau presented Moscheles with two such works: a riddle canon and a canon for two flutes for Professor G[uillou] since he regarded Moscheles's

[10] Letter to Andreas Kuhlau, 18 June 1829, in Busk, 135.

[11] Ibid., 75.

[12] Ignaz Moscheles, *Aus Moscheles' Leben*, 2 vols. (Leipzig: Duncker & Humblot, 1872-73), 1:213.

piano performances as a "lofty delight."[13] Assuming that this canon for two flutes is still extant, it might actually be the third movement of Kuhlau's flute Duo, op. 39, no. 3, but if this is not the case, then it must have disappeared forever among the scores of Guillou.

Between mid-November 1829 and 23 January 1830, Anton Bernhard Fürstenau, Kuhlau's flutist friend from Dresden to whom he dedicated the Duos, op. 39, was in Copenhagen, and just as during his first visit in 1823 he again presented concerts. On 27 December 1829 he performed among other pieces one of his recent compositions, a set of variations on "Dybt i havet" from Kuhlau's *Elverhøj*,[14] written as a tribute to his German-Danish composer friend. Fürstenau had heard the folk song either in one of the *Elverhøj* performances or in Kuhlau's own variations in the Duo, op. 102, no. 2, the score of which Kuhlau must have loaned him to "play through."

Fürstenau also tried out at that time Kuhlau's latest flute composition, *3 Duos brillants, für Klavier und Flöte oder (Violine)*, op. 110, which Kuhlau had composed between the middle of November and the middle of December 1829.[15] Since the duos were published by Farrenc in Paris, the work in question can only be *3 Sonaten für Pf. und Fl.* announced by Kuhlau on 25 April 1829,[16] and which earlier he had promised his publisher to write after the desired rest from composing for the flute. The title, *Duos brillants*, can be explained by the following: Originally Farrenc commissioned duos for two flutes, and for this reason Kuhlau called the piece "duo brillant," but it was really a sonata-form work for piano and flute. The compositional quality of op. 110, contrary to the other flute pieces of 1829, is so extraordinary that one must conclude that Kuhlau put to use here the most valuable experiences of his journey. Besides these duos, only one other important work was written under the impressions of his German trip of 1829, the G-minor Quartet for piano, violin, viola, and cello, op. 108, which was described by Moscheles during his visit as an "exceptional work."[17]

The Duos, op. 110, in three movements, are more compressed in their form than Kuhlau's previous grand flute sonatas. The structural elements are developed without great detours and retarding transitions, and with the virtuoso elements remaining in the background. The subtitle "brillant" refers not to the technical but the tonal presence demanded to the highest degree of both instruments. All three Duos of op. 110 present therefore a test of the interpretative ability of even advanced chamber music performers.

---

[13] Letter to Moscheles, 18 November 1829, in Busk, 144-45.

[14] Busk, 81.

[15] Ibid., 147ff.

[16] Letter to Farrenc, 25 April 1829, in Busk, 127-28.

[17] Moscheles, 1:213.

On 1 August 1830 Kuhlau sent his op. 110, published by Farrenc, to Baroness M. v. Schwerin, to whom the work is dedicated:

> Your Excellency Madame Baroness! I hope I can rely on your kind indulgence for my dedicating the enclosed work to your esteemed name. I would be extremely happy if Your Excellency would graciously accept this dedication provided that my work does not entirely displease you, and that you consider this as a small (perhaps insignificant) token of my highest esteem for you. Respectfully Yours.

When Kuhlau wrote this letter the pleasant times of the busy year of 1829 were but a memory. In the following years of 1830 and 1831 he was subjected to three fateful tragic events from which he would never recover.

11

Lyngby-Copenhagen, 1830-32: Trio, op. 119

Kuhlau spent the winter of 1829-30 in Lyngby, where in "rural peace" he wanted to dedicate himself complete to his "musical ideas."[1] He wrote to Baroness Schwerin "I have had to give up getting informed. . .,"[2] which indicates that at this time—with the exception of a visit by Fürstenau—Kuhlau withdrew more and more from the public cultural life of Copenhagen.

The first fatal blow came with the sudden and unexpected death of his father on 21 January 1830, which increased the loneliness of this man who had never married. His father died "without having been sick even in the smallest way."[3] He was 82 years old, an unusually old age for those times. Kuhlau, who had spent seventeen years in Denmark with his parents, had gotten used to family life, and now it dawned upon him that this life would not last forever. He now concentrated his entire concern for his mother who, at the beginning, survived the fatal blow relatively well. He wrote to Andreas on 27 March 1830:

> Our old mother, thank God, is quite well. Her memory though is so weak, that she has almost forgotten her blessed husband, and she has no time to think of him either, because all day she is busying herself with either the household or the chicken coop. She knows nothing of boredom, and thus she stays happy and healthy. I hope that she will live for many more years, and just to please her, I am not going to go away this summer.

---

[1] Letter to a baroness, probably M. v. Schwerin, 17 December 1829, in Busk, *Kuhlau Breve*, 149.

[2] Ibid.

[3] Letter to Andreas Kuhlau, 23 January 1830, in ibid., 154.

That summer Kuhlau really did stay home as much as he could, and on 21 June 1830 his sister, the widow Amalie Kuhlau-Jepsen, known as "Male," arrived in Lyngby to assist her brother and their mother. During this time Kuhlau wrote his last dramatic work, the theater music to *Trillingbrødrene fra Damask* (The Triplet Brothers of Damascus). After the great success of *Elverhøj*, for which Kuhlau was granted a double salary, the theater directors insisted that the season of 1830 should be opened by a new play with Kuhlau's music. In January Kuhlau rejected the libretto of *Raven* by Hans Christian Andersen (1805-75),[4] and for a while he also refused to write the music to *Trillingbrødrene* for lack of time.[5] The emphatic plea of the librettist finally changed his mind. It was Oehlenschläger, Kuhlau's dear friend, who wanted to see his new play performed with Kuhlau's music. On 23 April 1830 Kuhlau asked Oehlenschläger for the libretto, and finished the composition by August. The work consists of an overture, stanzas of songs, and chorus pieces. The premiere took place on 1 September 1830, and as it was not a great success there were only two more performances. Oehlenschläger explained the failure in the following way:

> I can say that the *Trillingbrødrene fra Damask* with Kuhlau's beautiful music did not get the recognition that it deserved. The predicament came about mainly because it was difficult to find three actors who resembled each other to such an extent that one would have mistaken one for the other. One did not want to and could not use masks, and one did not think of the simplest solution such as sticking on beards, mustaches, noses, etc.—which would have created a semblance of similarity. Winslow was excellent as Babekan and Madame Wexschall played Lyra exceptionally well.[6]

On November 9, just four days after the last performance of *Trillingbrødrene*, Kuhlau was dealt another fateful blow: his mother died. How much he suffered from the death of his parents is apparent not only from his letters written to his brother Andreas, but also from his business correspondence in which he makes references again and again to the loss of his parents. "Kindly forgive me for not having responded sooner to your last esteemed letter, but the reason (for me very sad) is that within a time span of a few months, I have lost both of my parents," he wrote in a December 11 letter to Farrenc. "Two funerals in one year—it is too much!" he said in a letter of the same day to Böhme.

During this difficult time toward the end of 1830, Kuhlau was considering composing something again for the flute. He was thinking of a sonata for flute

---

[4] Letter to Edvard Collin, 12 January 1830, in ibid., 151.

[5] Letter to Conrad Frederik von Holstein, 3 April 1830, in ibid., 158-59.

[6] Oehlenschläger, 4:44ff.

and piano intended for the French flutist Hippolyte Camus (1796-?), and also a piano quartet with flute for his publisher Farrenc and his wife. He wrote to Farrenc:

> I am flattered to know that Mr. Hl. Camus, whom you have recommended to me as an excellent virtuoso on the flute, likes my compositions. I would be very pleased to follow your request to dedicate to him a Grande Sonata for flute and piano provided that you would be the publisher of this work. For a long time I have been toying with the idea of dedicating a work to you and your wife. What would you say to a grand quartet for piano, flute, viola (or violin), and cello?[7]

However, neither of these compositions were realized, very likely because Farrenc did not want to publish them. But when Kuhlau received an offer from the British publisher Christian Rudolph Wessel (1797-1885), who had become aware of Kuhlau's music through his *Duos brilliants,* op. 110, he accepted the offer to write a similar work for Wessel:

> I am in receipt of Your Excellency's esteemed letter of December 14 of this year, and I am pleased to learn that you like my sonatas (or duets) for piano and flute, and that you would be inclined to publish similar works by me.[8]

But even this composition did not come to fruition, at first because Kuhlau suffered another catastrophic blow on 5 February 1831. As his sister Amalie wrote to their brother Andreas:

> February 5 was a very unhappy day for us. A fire broke out in our neighbor's house around 5 o'clock in the evening, and since there was a very strong wind, and the houses in Lyngby have mostly thatched roofs, it did not take more than a quarter of an hour before our house went up in flames. In the short time there was not much that we could save, and Fritz's loss—mostly in musical scores, can't even be calculated. For a long time we stood on the street in the snow and cold and stared at the horrible scene.[9]

This fire in the house of the glassblower Nielsen Halberg, where Kuhlau lived at that time with his sister and with his dog, Presto, had grave consequences for his health. Because of his exposure to the bitter winter night, his gout and cold became so severe that on 8 March 1831 he had to be taken to the Friedrich Hospital in

---

[7] Letter to Farrenc, 11 December 1830, in Busk, 169-70.

[8] Letter to Wessel, 22 January 1831, in ibid., 170-71.

[9] Letter from Amalie Kuhlau to Andreas Kuhlau, 12 April 1831, in ibid., 189-90.

**KUHLAU, IN A LITHOGRAPH
PUBLISHED BY WESSEL IN 1831,
FROM A PASTEL DRAWING BY C. HORNEMANN**

Copenhagen. Along with poor health he also suffered financially because of the fire—the loss of several manuscripts, among them a second piano concerto and an almost completed method for basso continuo. Kuhlau was especially sad because his beloved dog, Presto, had been injured so badly in the fire that he died soon thereafter.[10]

During his stay in the hospital, his friends organized a benefit concert for the ailing composer on 1 May 1831, for which Weyse composed a song for four voices for Kuhlau's recovery.[11] After three months, on June 7, Kuhlau was released from the hospital. To convalesce he went back to Lyngby, where he and his sister had rented a new apartment. By July his health had improved to the point that he could go back to his work. He remembered the promised flute composition and wrote to Wessel:

---

[10] Thrane, 94.

[11] Busk, 87.

> Would Your Excellency excuse me for not having answered your esteemed letter of February 18 of this year, but a severe illness from which I suffered for more than seven months prevented me from writing . . . thus, I hope to be able to send to you this year a duet in F major as you wished.[12]

The promised Duet in F major became the *Premiere Grande Trio concertant, für 2 Flöten und Pianoforte,* op. 119, which Kuhlau sent to Wessel on 9 December 1831:

> Highly Esteemed Sir! Yesterday with the departing post I sent out my Opus 119 . . . to Shiller & Co., with the request to pass it on to you. I hope and wish that this composition may be to your liking. It is cheerful, brilliant, and yet isn't very difficult to play, just as you specified. Since I don't have a metronome, and I could not find one here, I was not able indicate the tempos. On the other hand, the music itself suggests them. And now I have a request for you: I have dedicated this trio to Herr Franz Steigerwald (in Würzburg), and I would like to ask you to publish this dedication not only on the title page but have it printed as part of the title (as I have it now in the manuscript) and to request this also from the co-publishers—in case you have any—in Germany, or wherever else this work will be published.[13]

However, this dedication to Franz Steigerwald never materialized. Instead, the first edition was dedicated to the flutist Jean Sedlatzek (1789-1866), and why this happened could not be established. Op. 119, is Kuhlau's last composition for flute, and one of his last works in general.

In outline, op. 119, in three movements, follows the *Duos brilliant,* op. 110, in style, as Wessel, who had commissioned the piece, had specified. In all three movements Kuhlau follows the same principle. The main theme is played first by the piano alone, then the two flutes repeat it, the piano joins in, and then they play together. In the slow second movement, Adagio patetico, the eight-measure period of the main theme is distributed in such a way that the first part is played by the piano alone, and the second part by the two flutes alone. This division of the theme lends the first eight measures of the second part the character of an introduction, in which not only the thematic material is introduced, but also the voices of the similar instruments are placed next to each other. For this combination of instruments, op. 119 is the most important work of the Romantic period. It exist also in another arrangement for flute, cello, and piano, which is just as worthwhile to be studied, in case one is looking for an alternative to Weber's famous G-minor Trio, op. 63.

---

[12] Letter to Wessel, 11 July 1831, in Busk, *Kuhlau Breve*, 174.

[13] Letter to Wessel, 10 December 1831, in ibid., 179-80.

During the second part of the year of 1831 Kuhlau composed, along with op. 119, several smaller piano pieces and his first string quartet. As he explained in a letter to Farrenc:

> One of the local wealthy merchants and music sponsors has asked me to compose for him six quartets for four string instruments, and since I have been thinking of trying myself in this sort of composition, I have accepted this commission with great delight.[14]

By January 1832 Kuhlau had finished only one of the series of six planned string quartets commissioned by the merchant Waagepaterson: the first in A minor, op. 122. This was his last composition.

At the end of February 1832 Kuhlau's health deteriorated, since his severe cold and gout had not been completely cured during his three-month stay in the hospital. After two weeks of lying sick in bed, he died on 12 March 1832 in his apartment in Copenhagen, Nyhaven 12, where he and his sister had moved from Lyngby in October 1831.[15] On March 13 Amalie Kuhlau wrote to Andreas:

> He is no more, our good brother Fritz. After a sickness of 14 days and a tough struggle he passed away quietly and calmly last night at a quarter to eight. The funeral is Friday and will be a festive occasion, since Fritz was loved and honored by so many here.[16]

The last document that exists in Kuhlau's handwriting is a letter to the merchant W. Scherres in Königsberg dated 28 February 1832, which again characteristically was about a flute composition:

> I am in receipt of Your Excellency's so flattering letter of January 28, and I have the honor to respond to your inquiry. So far as flute quintets are concerned, I have only written three of this genre, namely the op. 51. I have made a commitment to compose a number of quartets for string instruments (without a flute), and this is what I am diligently engaged in now. As soon as I have finished this work, I will very likely be interested in writing a flute quintet again, and I shall take the liberty of notifying you as soon as such a work is finished. I send my greetings to you and to all the friends of music in your city.
>
> With the highest regards, your obedient servant
> F[r. Kuhlau]

---

[14] Letter to Farrenc, 18 July 1831, in ibid., 176-77.

[15] Busk identifies Kuhlau's fatal illness as tuberculosis. See his booklet for the recording of Kuhlau's *Lulu* (Kontrapunkt 32009/11, 1988).—Ed.

[16] Letter from Amalie Kuhlau to Andreas Kuhlau, 13 March 1832, in Busk, *Kuhlau Breve*, 191.

LITHOGRAPH OF KUHLAU BY LUDWIG FEHR, SR.

Friedrich Kuhlau did not live to be forty-six years old. To show the importance of flute music in the short life of this musician has been the aim of this work. Almost a quarter of Kuhlau's total works consists of flute music without counting the multiple pieces within a single opus number. Obviously, not all these compositions are of the same high level. However, most of his flute music is of such high technical quality and tailored so much to the flute that Kuhlau, through a fusion of these two merits, created a voice of his own, which had hardly been reached by any other flute compositions of the Romantic age. This is the simple reason why Kuhlau's flute music, in contrast to his operas and chamber music works, has endured to this day in the recital halls of the world.

Flute Compositions by Friedrich Kuhlau

op. 10 (bis) Variationen und Capricen, flute (1806)
Nos. 1-6: *Flöten-Journal für Flöte solo*, vol. 1—Zimmermann
Nos. 1-12: Amadeus; Billaudot (1975)

op. 10 3 Duos concertants, 2 flutes (1813)
International (n.d.); Carl Fischer (1917); Billaudot (n.d.); Pacific, Mo.: Mel Bay (1994)

op. 13 3 Grand Trios concertants, 3 flutes, in D, g, F (1813)
International (1976); Billaudot (1978)

op. 13b 3 Duos brillants, 2 flutes (arrangement not original)
Billaudot (n.d.)

op. 38 3 Fantasias, flute (1821)
Billaudot (n.d.); Universal (1975); Presser (n.d.)

op. 39 3 Grand Duos, 2 flutes, in e, B-flat, D (1821)
Billaudot (n.d.); Schirmer (n.d.); Carl Fischer (n.d.); International (n.d.)

op. 51 3 Quintets, flute, violin, 2 violas, cello, in D, E, A (1822)
No. 1: Samfundet til Udgivelse af dansk Musik (København, 1961—out of print)
No. 2: ibid. (out of print)
No. 3: Kunzelmann (1980)

Edited by Anton Keyper for flute and piano
No. 1: Costallat (out of print)

No. 2: Grand Sonate concertante en mi majeur—Billaudot (1972)
No. 3: Grand Sonate concertante en la majeur—Billaudot (1972)

op. 57 3 Grand Solos, flute and piano ad lib., in F, a, G (1823)
Billaudot (n.d.); Peters (n.d.)

op. 57b 3 Duos, 2 flutes (arrangement not original)
Billaudot (n.d.)

op. 63 Introduction and Variations on a Theme from Weber's *Euryanthe*, flute and piano (1824)
Bärenreiter (1971); Presser (n.d.)

op. 64 Sonata in E-flat major, flute and piano (1824)
Billaudot (1969); Carl Fischer (1994)

op. 68 6 Divertissements, flute and piano ad lib. (1825)
Billaudot (n.d.); Carl Fischer (n.d.); International (1960); Presser (n.d.)

op. 69 Grand Sonata in G major, flute and piano (1825)
Zimmermann (1986)

op. 71 Sonata in E minor, flute and piano (1825)
Gran Duo en mi mineur—Billaudot (1971)

op. 79 Violin Sonata in F major (1927), arranged for flute and piano
Billaudot (1970); Presser (n.d.)

op. 80 3 Duos, 2 flutes, in G, C, e (1827)
Billaudot (n.d.); Carl Fischer (n.d.); International (n.d.)

op. 81 3 Duos, 2 flutes, in D, F, G (1827)
Billaudot (n.d.); Carl Fischer (1922); International (n.d.)

op. 83 3 Sonatas, flute and piano, in G, C, c (1827)
No. 1: Bärenreiter (out of print)
No. 2: Bärenreiter (out of print)
No. 3: Billaudot (1971)

op. 85 Grand Sonata concertante in A minor, flute and piano (1827)
Billaudot; Schott (1986)

op. 86 3 Grand Trios, 3 flutes, in e, D, E-flat (1827)
Billaudot (n.d.); Kalmus (n.d.)

op. 87 3 Grand Duos, 2 flutes, in A, g, D (1827)
Carl Fischer (n.d.); Schott (n.d.)

op. 90 Grand Trio in B minor, 3 flutes (1827)
Billaudot (1976); Schott (1981); Kalmus (n.d.); International (1974)

op. 94 Variations on a Theme from Onslow's *Le Colporteur*, flute and piano (1828)
Zimmermann (1994)

op. 95 3 Fantasies, flute and piano ad lib., G, e, D (1824)
No. 1: Billaudot (1975); Zimmermann
No. 2: Billaudot (1975); Zimmermann
No. 3: Billaudot (1975); Zimmermann

op. 98 Introduction and Rondo on "Ah! quand il géle" from Onslow's *Le Colporteur*, flute and piano (1829)
Billaudot; Zimmermann

op. 99 Introduction and Variations on "Toujours de mon jeune âge" from Onslow's *Le Colporteur*, flute and piano (1829)
Zimmermann (1995)

op. 101 Introduction and Variations on a Theme from Spohr's *Jessonda*, flute and piano (1829)
Zimmerman (1995)

op. 102 3 Duos brillants, 2 flutes, in D, E, A (1827)
Billaudot (n.d.); Carl Fischer (n.d.); International (n.d.)

op. 103 Grand Quartet in E minor, 4 flutes (1829)
Billaudot (n.d.); Peters (n.d.); Ashdown (n.d.); Costallat (n.d.)

op. 104 Variations on a Scottish Folksong, flute and piano (1829)
Billaudot (1971); Presser (n.d.)

op. 105 Variations on an Irish Folksong, flute and piano (1829)
Billaudot (1975); Universal (1977); Presser (n.d.); Wiener Querflöten Edition (n.d.)

op. 110 3 Duos brillants, flute and piano, in B-flat, e, D (1820)
Billaudot (n.d.)

op. 119 Grand Trio in G major, 2 flutes and piano (or flute, cello, piano) (1831)
International (1977); Zimmermann (1990); Billaudot (1978); Costallat (1980); M. R. Braun (1960)

Bibliography

1. Reference Works

Baumgartner, Alfred. *Barok-Musik.* Der Grosse Musik Führer. Salzburg: Kiesel Verlag, 1981.
DTV Atlas zur Weltgeschichte. Edited by Herrmann Kinder and Werner Hilgemann. 22nd ed. Munich: Deutscher Taschenbuch Verlag, 1987.
Das grosse Handbuch der Oper. Edited by Heinz Wagner. Wilhelmshaven: F. Noetcel, 1987.
Das grosse Lexikon der Musik. Edited by Marc Honegger and Gunther Massenkeil. 10 vols. Freiburg in Breslau: Herder, 1978-83.
Herders Musiklexikon. Edited by Gerhard Hellwig. Freiburg: Herder, 1972.
Meyers Grosses Taschen-Lexikon. Edited and adapted by Meyer Lexikonredaktion. 2nd ed. Mannheim: Meyer, 1987.
Die Musik in Geschichte und Gegenwart (MGG). Edited by Friedrich Blume. 17 vols. Kassel: Bärenreiter, 1949-67. Taschenbuch edition. Munich: Deutscher Taschenbuch Verlag, 1989.
The New Grove Dictionary of Music and Musicians (1980). S.v. "Kuhlau, (Daniel) Friedrich [Frederik] (Rudolph)," by Carsten Hatting, with work-list and bibliography by Dan Fog.
Reclams Opernführer. Edited by Wilhelm Zentner. 25th ed. Stuttgart: Ph. Reclam, 1969.
Ullstein Lexikon der Musik. Edited by Friedrich Herzfeld. 8th ed. Frankfurt am Main: Verlag Ullstein, 1976.

2. Individual Books

Abendroth, Walter. *Schopenhauer.* Reinbek bei Hamburg: Rowohlt, 1967, 1984.
Alte schwedische Volks-Melodien. Gesammelt von E. G. Geijer und A. A. Afzelius. Copenhagen: C. C. Lose, 1818.

Beethoven, Ludwig van. *Ludwig van Beethovens Konversationshefte.* Edited by Karl-Heinz Köhler and Grita Herre. 9 vols. Leipzig: VEB Deutscher Verlag für Musik, 1968-88.

———. *Ludwig van Beethoven's Studien im Generalbass, Contrapunkt und Comositionslehre.* Edited by Ignaz Ritter von Seyfried. Vienna: T. Haslinger, 1832.

Boehm, Theobald. *Die Flöte und das Flötenspiel.* Munich: J. Aibl, 1871.

Burney, Charles. *Tagebuch einer musikalischen Reise durch Frankreich und Italien, durch Flandern, die Niederlande und am Rhein bis Wien, durch Böhmen, Sachsen, Brandenburg, Hamburg und Holland 1770-1772.* Edited by Eberhardt Klemm. Taschenbücher zur Musikwissenschaft, 65. Wilhelmshaven: Heinrichshofen, 1980. Originally published in English as *The Present State of Music in France and Italy* (London, 1771) and *The Present State of Music in Germany, the Netherlands, and United Provinces* (London, 1773), and soon translated to German by Christophe Daniel Ebeling and Johann Joachim Christoph Bode.

Busk, Gorm. *Friedrich Kuhlau: En biografi og en kritisk analyse af hans musikdramatiske produktion.* Diss., Kobenhavns Universitet. Aarhus: Publimus; Engstrøm & Sødring, 1986.

———. *Kuhlau breve, wie all folgenden Kuhlaubriefe.* Copenhagen: Engstrøm & Sødring, 1990.

———. Program notes to recording *Lulu,* by Friedrich Kuhlau. Klampenborg, Denmark: Kontrapunkt 32009/11, 1989, 1986.

Cammarota, Robert M. Program notes to recording *Flötenquintette, op. 51, nos. 1-3,* by Friedrich Kuhlau. CBS mk 44517, 19?.

Christiansen, Asgar Lund. Program notes to recording *Steichquartett op. 122,* by Friedrich Kuhlau. Dansk Musik Antologi DMA 090, 1969, 1988.

Dömling, Wolfgang. *Hector Berlioz in Selbstzeugnissen und Bilddokumenten.* Reinbek bei Hamburg: Rowohlt, 1977.

Einstein, Alfred. *Mozart: Sein Charakter, sein Werk.* Stockholm: Bermann-Fischer, 1947. Reprint, Frankfurt a.M.: Fischer Taschenbuch, 1980.

Fairbanks, Ann Kozuch. "Music for Two, Three, and Four Flutes by Friedrich Kuhlau." Ph.D. diss., Ohio State University, 1975.

Fog, Dan. *Kompositionen von Fridr. Kuhlau: Thematisch-bibliographischer Katalog.* Copenhagen: Dan Fog Musikverlag, 1977.

———. Program notes to recording *Elverhøj,* by Friedrich Kuhlau. Da Capo DCCD 8902, 1990.

Friedell, Egon. *Kulturegeschichte der Neuzeit: Die Krisis der europäischen Seele von der schwarzen Pest bis zum Ersten Weltkrieg.* Ungekürzte Ausg. in zwei Bänden. 6. Aufl. Vol. 2. Munich: Deutscher Taschenbuch-Verlag, 1986.

Goldberg, Adolph. *Porträts und Biographien hervorrangender Flöten-Virtuosen, -Dilettanten und -Komponisten.* Berlin, 1906; reprint, Celle: Moeck Verlag, 1987.

Graupner, Karl. *Friedrich Kuhlau.* Ph.D. diss., Universität München, 1930; Remscheid: Hermann Kromm, 1930.

Greither, Aloys. *Wolfgang Amadé Mozart in Selbstzeugnissen und Bilddokumenten.* Reinbek bei Hamburg: Rowohlt, 1962, 1976.

Häussermann, Ulrich. *Friedrich Hölderlin in Selbzeugnissen und Bilddokumenten.* Reinbek bei Hamburg: Rowohlt, 1961.

Hase-Schmundt, Ulrike von. Program notes to recording *Zwei Sonaten für Flöte und Klavier*, by Friedrich Kuhlau. Thun, Switzerland: Claves 50-8705, 1987.

Hildesheimer, Wolfgang. *Mozart.* Frankfurt a.M.: Suhrkamp, 1977.

Hodgson, Antony. Program notes to recording *Klavierkonzert op. 7, Concertino op. 45*, by Friedrich Kuhlau. Unicorn Dkp 9110, 1991.

Hoyer, Galina (Kiuriagina) von. *Tschaikowskij: Schicksal und Schaffen.* Vienna: Neff, 1972.

Hummel, Walter. *W. A. Mozarts Söhne.* Kassel: Bärenreiter, 1956.

Kölbel, Herbert. *Von der Flöte.* 3rd ed. Kassel: Bärenreiter, 1987.

Meylan, Raymond. *Die Flöte: Grundzuge ihrer Entsicklung von der Ürgeschichte bis zur Gegenwart.* 2. Aufl. Bern: Hallweg Verlag, 1975.

Moscheles, Ignaz. *Aus Moscheles' Leben.* 2 vols. Leipzig: Duncker & Humblot, 1872-73.

Moser, Hans Joachim. *Lehrbuch der Musikgeschichte.* Berlin: M. Hesse, 1937.

Oehlenschläger, Adam Gottlob. *Lebenserinnerungen.* Munich: G. Müller, 1923, 1925.

Ortheil, Hanns-Josef. *Jean Paul: Mit Selbstzeugnissen und Bilddokumenten.* Reinbek bei Hamburg: Rowohlt, 1984.

Ottenberg, Hans-Günter. *Carl Philipp Emanuel Bach.* Leipzig: P. Reclam, 1982.

Paul, Jean. *Flegeljahre: Eine Biographie.* Frankfurt a. M.: Insel, 1986.

Paumgartner, Bernard. *Mozart.* 8th ed. Zürich: Atlantis, 1980.

Pesek, Ursula and Zeljko. *Flötenmusik aus drei Jahrhunderten: Komponisten, Werke, Anregunen.* Kassel: Bärenreiter, 1990.

Pierreuse, Bernhard. *Flute Litterature.* Paris: Société des Editions Jobert, 1982.

Rachmanowa, Alja (pseud.). *See* Hoyer, Galina (Kiuriagina) von.

Reidemeister, Peter. Foreword to Friedrich Kuhlau, *Variations et caprices*, op. 10. Winterthur: Amadeus, 1981.

Rexroth, Dieter. *Beethoven: Leben—Werke—Dokumente.* 2nd ed. Mainz: Schott, 1988.

Scheck, Gustav. *Die Flöte und ihre Musik.* Mainz: Schott, 1975.

Scherliess, Volker. *Gioacchino Rossin: mit Selbstzeugen und Bilddokumenten.* Reinbek bei Hamburg: Rowohlt, 1991.

Schmid, Manfred Hermann. *Theobald Boehm: Die Revolution der Flöte.* Tutzing: Schneider, 1981.

Schmitz, Hans-Peter. *Flötenlehre.* Vol. 2. Kassel: Bärenreiter, 1955.

______. *Fürstenau heute.* Kassel: Bärenreiter, 1988.

Seidat, Hans E., ed. *Der Landkreis Uelzen.* Uelzen, 1981.

St. Bricka, Georgt. "Vorwort," in *Musik til William Shakespeare: Romantisk skuespil af C. J. Boye, op. 74.* Samfundet til udgivelse af dansk musik, ser. 1, no. 3. Copenhagen: Samfundet til udgivelse af dansk musik, 1873.

Thayer, Alexander Wheelock. *Ludwig van Beethoven's Leben.* 5 vols. Reprint, 2nd ed. Hildesheim: G. Olms, 1970-72. Originally published (in German), 1872-79; trans. to English, 1921. Rev. Elliot Forbes as *The Life of Ludwig van Beethoven.* 2 vols. Princeton: Princeton University Press, 1964.

Thrane, Carl. *Friedrich Kuhlau, deutsche Übersetzung aus "Danske Komponister."* Leipzig: Breitkopf und Härtel, 1886.

Vester, Frans. Foreword to Friedrich Kuhlau, *Fantasias*, op. 38. London: Universal Edition, 1975.

Wagner, Richard. *Das Rheingold: Der Ring des Nibelungen.* Text und Erläuterungen, edited by Kurt Pahlen. Munich, 1982.
Zobeley, Fritz. *Ludwig van Beethoven.* Reinbek bei Hamburg: Rowohlt, 1965.

Newspapers

Hamburgischer Correspondent. 17-28 November 1810.
Allgemine musikalische Zeitung 47 (November 1828).
Abendzeitung-Wochenend-Magazin. November 1986.

Libraries

Bayreuth (Thurnau), Berlin, Hamburg, Munich.

Archive

U.A. von Frau Marianne Henkel-Adorjan (Munich) und Herrn Zeljko Pesek (Tübingen).

3. MUSIC SCORES (flute compositions by Kuhlau are in a separate listing)

Beethoven, Ludwig van. *Variationen über Volksweisen für Klavier allein oder mit Begleitung einer Flöte ad lib.*, op. 105, 107. Wiener Urtext Edition, 1973.
———. *Quartett no. 15, A-moll, für 2 Violinen, Viola und Violoncell*, op. 132. Leipzig: Eulenburg, 193-?.
Boehm, Theobald. *Nel cor più*, variations, flute and piano, op. 4. Paris: Billaudot, 1972.
Kuhlau, Friedrich. *Elverhøj: Skuespil i fem acter*, op. 100. Reprint of Copenhagen: C. C. Lose, 1829. Musicus danicus, 4. Copenhagen: Dan Fog Musikforlag, 1978.
———. *Lulu: Romantische Oper in drei aufzügen.* Copenhagen: C. C. Lose, 1825.
———. *Sonatinen für zwei Händen*, op. 20. New York: Peters, 1900, 1989.
Möller, Herinrich, ed. *Skandinavische (Schwedische, Norwegische, Dänische, Isländische) Volkslieder.* Mainz: B Schott's Söhne, 1984.
———, ed. *Keltische (Bretonische, Kyrmische, Schottische, Irische) Volkslieder.* Mainz: B. Schott's Söhne, 1984.
Mozart, Wolfgang Amadeus. *Don Giovanni*, K. 527. London: Eulenburg, n.d.
———. *Le nozze di Figaro*, K. 492. London: Eulenburg. 1963.
———. *Die Zauberflöte*, K. 620. London: Eulenburg, 1984; piano score, New York: Peters, 1932.
Onslow, Georges. *Le Colporteur (Der Hausirer): Opéra comique en 3 actes.* Part, Bibliothek Bayreuth. Full score, Paris: Pleyel, 1827.
Paisiello, Giovanni. *Die schöne Müllerin: Komisches Singspiel in zwei Aufzügen.* Piano score. Berlin: E.H.G. Christiani, 1809.
Reinecke, Carl. *Undine: Sonate für Pianoforte und Flöte*, op. 167. Bad Godesberg: Forberg, 1967.
Schneider, Friedrich. *Sonate e-moll für Klavier und Querflöte,* op. 35. Kassel: Bärenreiter, 1987.
———. *Sonate in G-Dur für Klavier und Querflöte*, op. 33. Kassel: Barenreiter, 1987.

Silcher, Friedrich. *Variationen über "Nel cor non mi sente," für Flöte und Klavier.* Kassel: Bärenreiter, 1960.

Spohr, Louis. *Jessonda: Oper in drei Akten.* Piano score. Leipzig: C. F. Peters, 1879.

Vanhal, Johann Baptist. *Sechs Variationen über das Thema "Nel cor non mi sente," für Flöte (Violine) und Gitarre*, op. 42. Mainz: B. Schott's Söhne, 1977.

Weber, Carl Maria von. *Trio für Pianoforte, Violine, Violoncell*, op. 63. Leipzig: C. F. Peters, 1961.

Index

Translators

Lazslo M. Tikos, professor emeritus of Slavic Studies at the University of Massachusetts-Amherst, holds a M.A. from the University of Decrecen, Hungary (1954), and a Ph.D. from the University of Tübingen in Germany (1962). A former director of the University of Massachusetts Translation Center and president of Amherst Language Services, he is the author of *Gogol's Art: A Search for Identity* (Leverett, Mass.: BATI, 1997), and he has been a conference interpreter for Hungarian and German for the U.S. State Department since 1984.

Doris Tikos, a native German speaker, has been a piano teacher, accompanist extraordinaire, and church organist for the last twenty years.

Editor

Jane M. Rausch earned a B.A. at DePauw University, and a M.A. and Ph.D. at the University of Wisconsin in Madison. She joined the History Department at the University of Massachusetts-Amherst in 1969, where she teaches Latin American history. She is the author or editor of several books including *A Tropical Plains Frontier: The Llanos of Colombia 1531-1831* (Albuquerque: University of New Mexico Press, 1984); *The Llanos Frontier in Colombia History, 1830-1930* (same publisher, 1993); and *Colombia: Territorial Reform and the Llanos Frontier* (University Press of Florida, 1999) — the third in her set of books dealing with the region of tropical plains in that country. A serious amateur flutist for over four decades, she has a special fondness for early Romantic music.